Python

This Book Includes:

The Guide for Beginners, Machine Learning

By
Josh Hugh Learning

Josh Hugh Learning

Disclaimer Notice:

Please note the information contained within this document is for educational and entertainment purposes only. All effort has been executed to present accurate, up to date, and reliable, complete information. No warranties of any kind are declared or implied. Readers acknowledge that the author is not engaging in the rendering of legal, financial, medical or professional advice. The content within this book has been derived from various sources. Please consult a licensed professional before attempting any techniques outlined in this book.

By reading this document, the reader agrees that under no circumstances is the author responsible for any losses, direct or indirect, which are incurred as a result of the use of information contained within this document, including, but not limited to, — errors, omissions, or inaccuracies.

Python for Beginners

A Step by Step Guide to Python Programming, Data Science, and Predictive Model. A Practical Introduction to Machine Learning with Python.

by

Josh Hugh Learning

Table of Contents

Introduction

The following chapters will discuss all of the things that you need to learn in order to handle Python as a coding language, and how it can work with machine learning, and a lot of other topics, making it easier for you to really work on putting both of these together. If you are brand new to Python coding, and you want to be able to learn some of the basics of Python and then want to combine it together with machine learning, then this is the guidebook for you.

The first part of this guidebook is going to focus on the Python language. This is going to head through all of the different things that you are able to do when it comes to learning the Python code. We will look at what Python is all about, how you can choose this language over some of the others, and even some of the basic parts of coding in Python that you are able to work with. We will explore how the classes and objects work, how to focus on inheritances, exceptions, conditional statements, functions, variables, and more. This will help us to gain some of the basis that we need to start coding in Python, even if you have never been able to do this before.

Once we have gotten a good handle on some of the different things that we can do with the basics of Python, it is time to move on to some of the more intermediate and even advanced things that we are able to do with our Python language, and maybe a little bit of machine learning added to the mix. We are going to look at how we can create some of our own modules, with an example of how to do this, how to do the process of multithreading, how to access our database with the use of Python, and a good look at GUI programming.

To end this guidebook, we are going to spend our time doing an introduction to machine learning and some of the amazing things that you are able to do with machine learning. The technology world is booming with the idea of machine learning and you will be able to use this along with Python to see a lot of new things show up in your coding. This section will take some time to introduce machine learning and more of what it is about.

Working with the Python language is one of the best steps that you can take to improve your coding, and even to work with some machine learning down the line if you would like. When you are ready to learn more about how to start with Python coding as a beginner, and even some of the more advanced coding techniques that will bring you into the world of machine learning, then this is the guidebook for you!

There are plenty of books on this subject on the market, thanks again for choosing this one! Every effort was made to ensure it is full of as much useful information as possible, please enjoy!

Chapter 1: The Python Language

There are a lot of different options that you are able to work with when it comes to the world of coding. Coding is not always going to be as easy as it may seem and you have a lot of options based on what you would like to do, what kind of power you want to use, and even the operating system that seems to match up with your needs the best. But one of the program's languages that many programmers like to use, for a variety of reasons but especially when they want to do things that have to do with machine learning, is Python.

Python is an object-oriented programming language that is taking the world by storm. Programmers from all over the world, and with a lot of different experience levels when it comes to programming, are working with this language because they find it easy to work with, it has a lot of power, it is one of the must use languages with machine learning and other parts of data science, and there is a large community to ensure that you are able to use it for your needs. There are a lot of benefits that come with using this kind of language for your needs and we are going to talk about a few of them now.

Python is a good language for beginners. One of the main reasons that a lot of programmers like to go with Python is because it is designed with the beginner in mind. The library is simple to use, reading through the codes is easy even if you haven't learned a single thing about doing stuff in Python, and you get the added benefit of having an object oriented coding language so you will get the code to work for your needs, even when you are just starting out. If you have ever wanted to get into the world of programming and coding, then Python is one of the best programming languages to work with.

Python can bring in a lot of power to your codes. We just spent some time talking about how the Python coding language is all about being the perfect one to use for beginners. But this doesn't mean that you are going to sacrifice computing power and strength of your codes simply because of the fact that this language was designed with beginners in mind.

In fact, a lot of people who have been working on programming for years are going to enjoy learning how to use this language as well because of the amount of power and strength that comes with it. Even as a beginner language, Python has the capabilities to handle a lot of the different things that you want to do with coding. From handling machine learning to doing data science and more, Python is definitely the language that will help you to get it all done.

Python is also going to have a large library that you are able to work with. While there are a lot of benefits that come with other coding languages, you will certainly enjoy working with Python and all that it is able to provide inside of its library. And when you need to do something like machine learning and artificial intelligence that is not found in the traditional Python library, you will be able to easily change things up and add in one of the extensions to make this work for your needs as well.

There is a large community that goes with Python. Because Python is such a well-known language, and because there is a lot of ease that comes with using this language and a lot of power, along with a lot of things that you are able to do when you choose this language a large community around the world has started to make sure you can get things done.

The program is open-sourced. This means that you won't have to worry about someone taking over the code and ruining it. It also means that the original Python is free and available to anyone who wants to download it. Of course, there are some parties that have taken parts of Python and developed them to meet certain specifications and then try to sell them. But you can always just work with the basics of the Python code without having to purchase anything else to get the program and its components to work.

There are a lot of different ways that you can benefit from this community. You will find that this community will be able to show you some of the cool things that you can do with Python, help you to progress your codes more, and even help you out when you have a question or something in your code is not working the way that you would like.

Python is going to provide you with a lot of integration features. Python can be great because it integrates what is known as the Enterprise Application Integration. This really helps with a lot of the different things you want to work on in Python including COBRA, COM, and more. It also has some powerful control capabilities, as it calls directly through Java, C++, and C. Python also has the ability to process XML and other markup languages because it can run all of the modern operating systems including Windows, Mac OS X, and Linux through the same kind of byte code.

Python provides more productivity for the programmer. The Python language has a lot of designs that are object-oriented and a lot of support libraries. Because of all these resources and how easy it is to use the program, the programmer is going to increase their productivity. This can even be used to help improve the productivity of the programmer while using languages like C#, C++, C, Perl, VB, and even Java.

This language will work on all of the operating systems. Another thing that a lot of people like about working with Python is that it helps them to create codes in any kind of operating system they want to use. You are not going to be limited based on what kind of computer you are on and what operating system you would like to use the most based on preference. You can easily visit www.python.org in order to pick out which operating system you want to use and then download the version of Python that matches up to this.

Python and machine learning are able to work together to complete some powerful codes. There are a lot of really neat things that you are able to do when you decide to work with the Python language. While you may need to add in a few extensions and libraries to get it done, you will be able to use the basics of the Python code, along with some of the stuff that we discuss in this guidebook to make those powerful codes run. If you have been working with machine learning or interested in learning how to do this, you will find that Python is the perfect language to use to make it happen.

There are a lot of things that you are going to enjoy when it comes to the Python coding language. There may be a lot of other languages out there that can help you to get things done when you are coding, but none are going to be as efficient, as easy to use, and as powerful as the Python language, and this is exactly why so many people choose to add this into their toolbelt when they want to learn a new coding language.

Installing the Python program

Another thing that we need to spend some time looking at is installing your Python program so that you can begin writing out some of the codes that are needed with this kind of language. There are some simple steps that you can take in order to get started with this kind of coding language, and it can be as easy or as difficult to work with as you choose.

Python is going to work on all of the coding languages, whether you are working with Linux, Windows, or the Apple systems. Sometimes, the Mac OS X is going to include version 2 of Python on it already, and you can certainly use this for your needs if you choose. But since most of the machine learning libraries work best with

Python 3, it is usually best to go through and add the newer versions on so you can do some of that more advanced work that can come up later.

If you check your system, usually with Linux or Mac OS X (Windows has its own coding language so it will not already have a version of Python on it unless you actively went through and did it yourself), and see that there is a version of Python already on there, you will either need to work with that one, or make sure to remove it off your system so that you can upload the new one and not have two programs that are fighting against each other.

Downloading the Python language that you want to work with is going to require a few steps, but luckily, working with the option from *www.python.org* can make this easier. You can choose to work with another place to get Python, but this website includes the IDE, the files, the compiler, and all of the other parts that you need to make the system work. If you go with another website, then it is possible that you are not going to get the right version of this in place, or that you will miss out on some of the files that you need, and then you have to do extra work.

When you visit *www.python.org*, you will just pick out the version of Python that you want, and which operating system you would like to work with. With this chosen, you can then go through and follow the steps that are needed to download it on any kind of operating system that you would like to use, whether it is for Windows, Linux, or your Mac operating system. It may take a bit of time, but after a few minutes, you will find that this is set up and ready to go for you, and all of the files and parts that you want will be there.

Keep in mind with this one that we are talking about the original files that come with Python. There are going to be a lot of different libraries and extensions that you may want to use later on, such as the machine learning libraries, that are not going to be included in this download. But these are simple to use and can be a lot of fun to work with as well, as long as you already have the Python basics downloaded on your system.
www.python.org

----------------- *Example for Windows*

1. Click to Python Download

2. Click the Windows link, the following page will appear in your browser.

Python >> Downloads >> Windows

Python Releases for Windows

- Latest Python 3 Release - Python 3.7.4
- Latest Python 2 Release - Python 2.7.16

Stable Releases

- Python 3.7.4 - July 8, 2019
  Note that Python 3.7.4 cannot be used on Windows XP or earlier.

  - Download Windows help file
  - Download Windows x86-64 embeddable zip file
  - Download Windows x86-64 executable installer
  - Download Windows x86-64 web-based installer
  - Download Windows x86 embeddable zip file
  - Download Windows x86 executable installer
  - Download Windows x86 web-based installer
- Python 3.6.9 - July 2, 2019
  Note that Python 3.6.9 cannot be used on Windows XP or earlier.

Pre-releases

- Python 3.8.0b3 - July 29, 2019
  - Download Windows help file
  - Download Windows x86-64 embeddable zip file
  - Download Windows x86-64 executable installer
  - Download Windows x86-64 web-based installer
  - Download Windows x86 embeddable zip file
  - Download Windows x86 executable installer
  - Download Windows x86 web-based installer
- Python 3.8.0b2 - July 4, 2019
  - Download Windows help file
  - Download Windows x86-64 embeddable zip file
  - Download Windows x86-64 executable installer
  - Download Windows x86-64 web-based installer
  - Download Windows x86 embeddable zip file

3. Click on the **Download,** the following pop-up window titled **Opening python-3.74-amd64.exe** will appear.

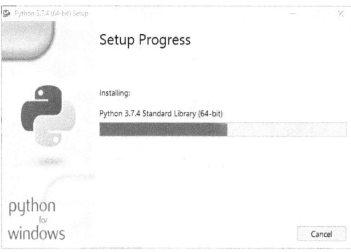

Writing your First Program

Now that we have had some time to explore what Python is all about and some of the benefits that come with it and before we move on to the different parts of the code and some other coding experiences that we can work with, we need to take some time to learn how to do a simple code in Python. This is something that a lot of different coding languages are going to work with as well and gives you a chance to explore Python a bit more, open up the compiler, and see how things are going to work inside of this language. So, let's dive in and see some of the steps that are needed to run our very own Hello, World! Program in Python.

To work with the Hello World! Program, you can open up your command line text editor. This should have come with the version of Python that you downloaded so open this up and create a new file. Inside, write out the following line:

$ nano hello.py

Once you get this text file to open up in your terminal window, you can then type out the program by writing out the following line:

print("Hello, World!")

Now that we have been able to write out some of the code, it is time to break it down into some of the different parts that come with the code. The print() function is going to be the part of the code that will tell the computer what action you would like it to perform. We know that this is a function thanks to the parenthesis that are there. This function is there in order to tell the compiler to display the information that you add into this part. By default, this is going to be the output that happens in the terminal window that is current for you.

Some of the functions, including the print function, are going to be ones that are, by default, found in the Python code. You can use them in any of the programs that you want to create and it is possible to add them in to create your very
own functions with the help of other elements that are found in the Python code.

When you are in the parentheses of this function, we wrote out the term "Hello, World!". This is going to be enclosed inside quotation marks. Any characters that we place into these quotation marks are called a string. Once we write down our program, we can exit the terminal by typing the control and the X keys, and then when you receive the prompt to save, the program will come up and you can just press y. Exiting will put you back in your shell.

Now that you have written out this program, you can run it in your program. We are going to work with the Python3 command along with the name that we gave the program file. To run the program, you can just write out the following line in your command prompt:

$ python3 hello.py

When you type this out into the command line, the terminal is going to give you the following output:

Hello, World!

Let's take a closer look over what happened in this program. Python went through and executed the line that said print("Hello, World!") by calling on the print() function like we talked about before. The string value was then passed over to the function.

For this example, your Hello, World! is known as the argument because the value is going to be passed over to a function. The quotes that we put on either side of this statement weren't printed on the screen here because they are simply there to tell Python that the function contains a string. These quotation marks are not part of the string; they are simply there to tell the compiler when the string starts and when it ends. Since the program is running, you know that you installed Python 3 properly on your system and that you wrote out the program in the right manner.

Congratulations! You have written out the Hello, World! Program in Python 3! You are now prepared to work on some of the other great programs that we will discuss in this guidebook!

Chapter 2: Data and Variables

Working on the Python code can be an exciting time. It allows you to write some strong and powerful codes that are also going to hold onto a lot of information and be easy enough for a beginner to work with. Data and variables are going to be a big part of this, and we need to take a look at how these work within our code. So, with this in mind, let's get started to see how these work together to create some of the basic codes that you need in Python.

The Keywords

As a programmer, it is a good idea to take some time to learn about the keywords that are going to show up in your code. These seem pretty simple, but if you do not put them in at all or you put them in at the wrong places, it is going to spell disaster when you are working on your code. These keywords are basically the commands that are sent over to your compiler to tell it what to do. As you can see from this, using them in the wrong manner is going to cause some issues.

If you don't put a keyword into the code, then your compiler is going to have no idea what its commands are and it won't know what to do next. If you put the keyword in the wrong place or try to use it in a different location than where it is meant to be, then it is likely that an error message is going to show up and you have to sort through the code to get things matched up again. It is best to learn what these keywords are from the beginning, and then make sure that things are in the right place so you can easily find them later.

Working with Variables

It is also important for us to take some time and look at how to work with the variables and data that come in this kind of language. These variables are basically anything in the code that is going to hold onto a changeable value. The variable is similar in idea to a box that is able to hold onto things. These are important to focus on at least a little bit because they are there to make sure that you can find them and then use a specific value that you need at a later time.

The main thing that we want to focus on when we are looking at these variables is how we are able to assign the right value over to it. To get the variable to behave the way that we want, you need to make sure that it has a value assigned to it. If the value is never assigned, then you are just making a variable that results in some empty space on the memory of your computer, and nothing is going to show up later when you try to use it. But, if you do take the time to assign a value to the variable and sometimes even more than one value to a variable, then the whole thing is going to work in the manner that you would like.

As you work with variables, you will find that there are actually three options that you can use. Each of them can be useful and it will depend on the type of code you are working on and the value that you want to assign to that particular variable. The variables that you are able to pick from will include:

- Float: this would include numbers like 3.14 and so on.

- String: this is going to be like a statement where you could write out something like "Thank you for visiting my page!" or another similar phrase.

- Whole number: this would be any of the other numbers that you would use that do not have a decimal point.

When you are working with variables in your code, you need to remember that you don't need to take the time to make a declaration to save up this spot in the memory. This is automatically going to happen once you assign a value over to the variable using the equal sign. If you want to check that this is going to happen, just look to see that you added that equal sign in, and everything is going to work.

Assigning a value over to your variable is pretty easy. Some examples of how you can do this in your code would include the following:

x = 12   *#this is an example of an integer assignment*
pi = 3.14   *#this is an example of a floating-point assignment*
customer name = John Doe   *#this is an example of a string assignment*

Another option that is available for the coder to work on here, and that we did mention a bit above, is that you can take two or more values and assign them over to the same variable. There are a few instances where this can be useful in the code that you are writing, so it is a nice thing to take a look at and learn how to do. It is easier than it may seem. You would simply need to go through the same kind of coding and procedure that we used above, but just make sure that the equal sign is showing up between the variable and the two values that are meant to be assigned to it.

How to Name your Identifiers

Your identifiers can be important to your code as well, and in Python, there are quite a few identifiers to work with too. You will find that they come in at a lot of different names and you may see them as functions, entities, variables, and classes. When you are naming an identifier, you can use the same information and the same rules will apply for each of them, which makes it easier for you to remember the rules.

The first rule to remember is when you name these identifiers. You have many options when you are naming your identifiers. For example, you can rely on both uppercase and lowercase letters with naming, as well as any number and the underscore symbol. You can also combine any of these together. One thing to remember here is that you can't start the name with a number and there shouldn't be any spaces between the words that you write out. So, you can't write out 3words as a name, but you can write out words3 or threewords. Make sure that you don't use one of the keywords that we discussed above or you will end up with an error.

When you pick out the identifier name, you can follow the rules above, and try to pick out a name that you can remember. Later on, when writing the code, you will need to pull it back up, and if you give it a name that is difficult to remember, you could run into problems or raise errors because things aren't showing up the way that you want. Outside of these rules, you will be fine naming the identifiers anything that you want.

The Operators

While we will take a closer look at these operators in a bit, especially the comparison operators, we are going to take a moment to look at some of the basics that come with these operators and how we are able to use them for our own benefit when writing out some codes in the Python language. They are simple to work with but add in a lot of power and capabilities to what you are doing in this language.

Operators are pretty simple parts of your code, but you should still know how they work. You will find that there are actually a few different types of them that work well. For example, the arithmetic functions are great for helping you to add, divide, subtract, and multiply different parts of the code together. There are assignment operators that will assign a specific value to your variable so that the compiler knows how to treat this. There are also comparison operators that will allow you to look at a few different pieces of code and then determine if they are similar or not and how the computer should react based on that information.

Adding in the Comments

The next thing that we need to take some time to look at is the comments that are in Python. These comments are going to be great little additions that come with the code that you are writing because they help you to leave a note or some information about what is happening in that part of the code, without having to really worry about the negative effects that come with adding it to the code. The compiler with Python is going to be set up in a manner that will ensure this is taken care of and that you can add in as many of these comments as you would like, without it having it show up in the code.

To make this work, you just need to add the # sign before you write out the comment. That sign is going to be enough to tell the compiler that you are working with a comment, and that it should just skip right over that thing, without reading it or having it interrupt the code that you are trying to write. It is that simple. You can technically add in as many of these as you would like to your code, but you should just keep it down to the things that are the most important to mention, not every little thing. This helps to make sure that the code is easier to read, that it is not too convoluted, and more.

Working with the data and some of the variables that come with the Python language can be a great way for you to get started with some of the codes that you have, but learning how to do all of these can take some time and effort to get done. When you are done with these though, you are going to be set to write out some of your own codes, and do some of the other exercises, that we are going to discuss in this guidebook.

Chapter 3: Control Flow Tools

The next thing that we can take a look at is some of the control flow tools that are available. There are a lot of different parts that you are able to add into your code to make sure that it can handle decisions, that you can deal with any errors that show up, and ensure that the program is going to work the way that you would like. Some of the different control flow tools that you can work with and can help you learn some of the basics of coding in Python include:

Comparison Operators

There are a lot of different types of operators that you are able to use based on what you would like to see happen in your code. The most common types of operators are going to be the arithmetic operators that allow you to add and subtract different parts of your code together. But the comparison operators can be an important part of the code. The comparison operators are going to make it possible to take at least two parts of the code and compare them to one another. You will have to use what is known as the Boolean expressions for this because you are going to get an answer that either says true or false. The parts of the code that you are comparing, for example, are either going to be the same, so true, or they will be different, which is false. There are a few operators that you will be able to work with that fit under the term of comparison operators which include:

- (>=): this one means to check if the left-hand operand is greater than or equal to the value of the one on the right.

- (<=): this one means to check if the value of the left-hand operand is less than or equal to the one on the right.

- (>): this one means to check whether the values of the left side are greater than the value on the right side of the code.

- (<): this one means to check whether the values of the left side are less than the values that are on the right side.
- (!=): this is the *not equal to* operator.

- (==): this one is *the equal to* operator.

The *if statements*

Conditional statements are going to be an important part of your code as well. These allow the program to make decisions, based on the conditions that you set. There are three different types of conditional statements that you are able to work with including the if statement, the if-else statement, and the elif statement. All of these are going to work in a similar manner, but it depends on how you would like the program to behave and what you want it to do.

Let's start with the if statement. This is the most basic out of the three, and it is not used as often because it missed on out a few things that you need. With this option, the user puts in an input that is either true or false based on the conditions that you set. If the answer is true, then your code will proceed. If the answer is false, then the code is going to stop because there is nothing there. An example of how this is going to work as code is to put the following code into your compiler and execute it:

```
age = int(input("Enter your age:"))
if (age <=18):
```

```
        print("You are not eligible for voting, try next
election!")
print("Program ends")
```

Then we need to take a look at the if-else statements. These follow the same idea that we saw with the if statements but takes it a bit further to handle what the user puts in, no matter the answer. You can keep it simple, with one result if the answer is true and another if it is false. Or you can allow for a range of answers, with a catch-all to catch any of the answers that you didn't include. For example, if you wanted the user to pick out their favorite color, you may include five color choices in the if-else statement, and then use the catch-all, or the else part of the code, to catch any other color the user would like to use.

We will start with a basic if-else statement, going off the idea that we did in the code above. This one will catch the age of the user whether they are younger than 18 or above. The code that you can use to have this happen includes:

```
age = int(input("Enter your age:"))
if (age <=18):
        print("You are not eligible for voting, try next
election!")
```

else

print("Congratulations! You are eligible to vote. Check out your local polling station to find out more information!)

print("Program ends")

And the third option that you are able to work with will be the elif statement. These can be compared to the menu option that you would see with a game. The user will be able to choose from a specific number of options, and then the code will proceed from there. The user can not just put in what they want; they have to choose one of the options that are given for the elif statement to work the way that you want.

Let's look at an example of how this will work. We are going to make our own menu that includes options for the user to chose which type of pizza they would like to eat. You can type in the following code to help you get this done:

Print("Let's enjoy a Pizza! Ok, let's go inside Pizzahut!")
print("Waiter, Please select Pizza of your choice from the menu")
pizzachoice = int(input("Please enter your choice of Pizza:"))

```
if pizzachoice == 1:
    print('I want to enjoy a pizza napoletana')
elif pizzachoice == 2:
    print('I want to enjoy a pizza rustica')
elif pizzachoice == 3:
    print('I want to enjoy a pizza capricciosa')
else:
    print("Sorry, I do not want any of the listed pizzas,
please bring a Coca Cola for me.")
```

Exceptions

Exceptions are a unique thing that you are able to add into your code. These are going to either be raised as a personal exception based on how things work in your particular code, or they could be a specific exception that Python raises because the user did something that is not allowed. A good example of this is when the user tries to divide by zero, or they try to use the wrong name, or the wrong spelling, to bring out a variable or a function later on.

Knowing how to raise these exceptions can be important when you are trying to work on your code. There is a lot that goes into them, but knowing how these work can give you some more control over the codes that you are writing, and can help you learn how to anticipate when these are going to show up, while also determining how you would like to handle them.

There is a lot that you are able to do when it comes to exceptions in your code, but we are going to focus on the meat of it and look at how you can raise some of your own exceptions. The basic code that we are going to be able to work with that ensures that you are able to deal with an error that shows up while making sure that you can leave a personalized message to the user so they know what they are aware of what problem is going on so they can fix it includes:

```
x = 10
y = 0
result = 0
try:
        result = x/y
        print(result)
except ZeroDivisionError:
        print("You are trying to divide by zero.")
```

You could choose to work on the code and not add in this personalized message, but this makes it easier. Most of the users you are going to deal with on your program are not going to be coders, and they will not understand what the long and drawn out error message is all about. With that in mind, being able to write it out and explain what is going on and how the user can fix it, like with the example above, can make things a bit easier on everyone.

The Inheritances

It is also important that we take a look at how some of these inheritances are going to work in the code that you work with. Working with an inheritance is a great way for you to have a chance to enhance a lot of the codes that can be created in Python. These inheritances are going to cut down on a lot of the time it takes to get things done while making sure that the code looks better and can run properly. Inheritances are going to be something that is new and unique to OOP languages so having them available in Python can be a nice perk.

Basically, when you decide to work with these inheritances, you will be able to take the first part of the code that you have, which we are going to call the parent code, and then move it down so you can make some changes to it, without messing with the original code that you were writing. You can do this without having anything change with the parent code while reusing and changing up the parts that you would like from the parent code.

To help us see how this kind of inheritance is going to work for us, we need to take a look at some of the code that you are going to be able to rely on when doing Python. Some example of coding that works well for this includes the following below:

```
#Example of inheritance
#base class
class Student(object):
        def__init__(self, name, rollno):
        self.name = name
        self.rollno = rollno
#Graduate class inherits or derived from Student class
class GraduateStudent(Student):
        def__init__(self, name, rollno, graduate):
        Student__init__(self, name, rollno)
        self.graduate = graduate

def DisplayGraduateStudent(self):
        print"Student Name:", self.name)
```

```
        print("Student Rollno:", self.rollno)
        print("Study Group:", self.graduate)
#Post Graduate class inherits from Student class
class PostGraduate(Student):
        def __init__(self, name, rollno, postgrad):
        Student__init__(self, name, rollno)
        self.postgrad = postgrad

        def DisplayPostGraduateStudent(self):
        print("Student Name:", self.name)
        print("Student Rollno:", self.rollno)
        print("Study Group:", self.postgrad)

#instantiate from Graduate and PostGraduate classes
        objGradStudent = GraduateStudent("Mainu", 1,
"MS-Mathematics")
        objPostGradStudent = PostGraduate("Shainu", 2,
"MS-CS")
        objPostGradStudent.DisplayPostGraduateStudent
()
```

When you type this into your interpreter, you are going to get the results:

('Student Name:', 'Mainu')

('Student Rollno:', 1)

('Student Group:', 'MSC-Mathematics')

('Student Name:', 'Shainu')

('Student Rollno:', 2)

('Student Group:', 'MSC-CS')

Functions

The next part of the code that we need to take a quick look at is going to be the Python functions. These functions are simply just a set of expressions and can be called statements in some cases, and are either going to be anonymous or have a name depending on what the programmer would like. These functions are going to be some of the objects that belong to the first class, which means that there aren't going to necessarily be a ton of restrictions on what you can use these for in the code.

With this said, you will find that there is a lot of diversity that comes with the functions and you are able to work with a lot of attributes to make these run. A few of the different attributes that work well with the Python functions will include:

- __doc__: This is going to return the docstring of the function that you are requesting.

- Func_default: This one is going to return a tuple of the values of your default argument.

- Func_globals: This one will return a reference that points to the dictionary holding the global variables for that function.

- Func_dict: This one is responsible for returning the namespace that will support the attributes for all your arbitrary functions.

- Func_closure: This will return to you a tuple of all the cells that hold the bindings for the free variables inside of the function.

The Loops

Loops are another important part of the code that we need to spend some time on. These are basically going to be a helpful part that cuts down on the actual number of lines of code that you need to write out at a time. If there is something in your code that you need to have repeated over again at least a few times, such as a chart or a table that you want to make, then the loop will come in and handle this for you. It saves time it makes the code look better and helps you to not have to write out as many lines of code.

There are going to be a few different types of loops that you are able to work with. The first kind is going to be the while loop. This is the one that a programmer would go with for their code when they already know how many times before they start. The code should go through and cycle with the loop. You may use this when you would like the code to count from one to ten because you know exactly when the loop needs to stop. A good example of how the code looks to make the loop show up would be the following:

```
#calculation of simple interest. Ask the user to input the
principal, rate of interest, number of years.
counter = 1
while(counter <= 3):
        principal   =   int(input("Enter   the   principal
amount:"))
        numberofyeras = int(input("Enter the number of
years:"))
        rateofinterest = float(input("Enter the rate of
interest:"))
        simpleinterest = principal * numberofyears *
rateofinterest/100
        print("Simple interest = %.2f" %simpleinterest)
        #increase the counter by 1
        counter = counter + 1
        print("You have calculated simple interest for 3
time!")
```

Now that we have a good idea of how the while loop
works, we need to take a look at the *for loop*. With this
one, you let the loop go as many times as it needs until
the input is done. This may be one time or it could be
ten times. When you work with these for loops, they will
not be the one who provides the code with the
information to get the loop to start. Instead, this loop is

going to complete an iteration in the order that you added it into the code and places it on the screen. There isn't really a need for the user to do this because the loop will just go through all of the iterations that you set up. The code example that you can use to see how this works includes:

```
# Measure some strings:
words = ['apple', 'mango', 'banana', 'orange']
for w in words:
print(w, len(w))
```

And finally, we are going to take a look at what is known as a nested loop. This one is going to work a bit differently than the other two in that it is going to have one loop that runs inside of another loop, and it is not done until both of these have reached the end. A good example of when you would want to use this kind of loop would be with a multiplication chart. You do not want to go through the code and write out one times one, and all the way up to ten times ten in order to create the code. A nested loop can take all of it down to just a few lines of code and still make the whole chart. What this would look like is the following:

```
#write a multiplication table from 1 to 10
For x in xrange(1, 11):
        For y in xrange(1, 11):
        Print '%d = %d' % (x, y, x*x)
```

When you got the output of this program, it is going to look similar to this:

1*1 = 1

1*2 = 2

1*3 = 3

1*4 = 4

All the way up to 1*10 = 10

Then, it would move on to do the table by twos such as this:

2*1 =2

2*2 = 4

And so on until you end up with 10*10 = 100 as your final spot in the sequence.

There is so much that you are able to do when you choose to write out codes in the Python language. This is definitely a language that takes some time to learn and you may have to experiment with some of the codes that come up to make sure that you are using them the proper way. But as it all comes together and you start to put some of these different parts together to form your own code, it will quickly make sense and you will be amazed at all of the things that you are able to do with the Python code.

Chapter 4: The Files

In this chapter, we are going to spend some time looking at how you can deal with the input and output of files within Python. There are a lot of different things that you are able to do with this, and you will need to be able to bring all of them out at some point or another as you are working on your code. The four things that we are going to look at is how to create a new file, how to close a file, how to look for and move a file, and how to write on a file that you have already created and saved.

Creating a new file

The first option that we are going to take a look at in this chapter is how to create a new file for your needs. If you would like to make a new file that you can write out code on, then you need to open up the IDLE and then choose the mode you want to use. There are going to be three modes that work with creating a file including mode(x), write(w), and append(a).

Any time that you are looking to make some changes to the file that you have opened, you want to use the write method because this one is easiest for you to use. And if you would like to open up a file and get a new string written in that file, you would also need to work with the write method. This ensures that everything goes in the right place and the characters are going to be returned by the compiler.

You will be able to use the write() function on a regular basis because it is easy and allows the programmer to come in and make any of the changes that they want to the file. You can add in some new information, change up some of the information you have, and so on. To look at how the code is going to appear in the compiler when you are working with the write() function, use the code below:

```
#file handling operations
#writing to a new file hello.txt
f = open('hello.txt', 'w', encoding = 'utf-8')
f.write("Hello Python Developers!")
f.write("Welcome to Python World")
f.flush()
f.close()
```

In addition to being able to create and write on a file that is brand new, there may be times when you need to go through and overwrite some of the information that you have to ensure that a new statement, or a new part, shows up that wasn't there before. Python does allow for it, and the code that you need to use to make this happen will be below:

```
#file handling operations
#writing to a new file hello.txt
f = open('hello.txt', 'w', encoding = 'utf-8')
f.write("Hello Python Developers!")
f.write("Welcome to Python World")
```

mylist = ["Apple", "Orange", "Banana"]

#writelines() is used to write multiple lines into the file

f.write(mylist)

f.flush()

f.close()

The next thing that we can work on doing is binary files. This is simple to do because it is going to take the data that you have and change it over to a sound or an image file instead of a text file. You are able to go through and change up any of the text that you want to write in Python, and then move it into the sound or image. The syntax that is going to make this possible includes:

 # write binary data to a file

 # writing the file hello.dat write binary mode

F = open('hello.dat', 'wb')

 # writing as byte strings

f.write(b"I am writing data in binary file!/n")

f.write(b"Let's write another list/n")

f.close()

Now that we have had a chance to create a file and even turn it into a binary file if it is needed, it is time to work with opening up a file to use again, after it has been closed, of course. There are times when you will want to open up the file and make some changes or work with the text in some way or another and opening up the file will help this to happen. The code that is going to make sure that you can get this done includes:

 # read binary data to a file

#writing the file hello.dat write append binary mode

with open("hello.dat", 'rb') as f:

data = f.read()

text = data.decode('utf-8'(

print(text)

The output that you would get from putting this into the system would be like the following:

Hello, world!

This is a demo using with.

This file contains three lines.

Hello, world!

This is a demo using with.

This file contains three lines.

And the final thing that we are going to look at doing here is how to seek out your file. This could help you to move your file over to a new location so it is easier to find and does the work that you need. For example, if you are working with a file and you find that things are not matching up the right way because you chose the wrong directory or spelled things in the wrong way, then you may need to work with the seek option in order to make sure that it can be fixed.

You have the ability to go through and change up where the file is located to make sure that the file ends up in the right spot, and to make it easier to bring it up and find it later on if it is needed. You just have to use the right input to tell the code where to place the file, and then make the changes to do this.

Working the files in this kind of language is going to be helpful when you are trying to get things to work out the right way in your code, when you want to make a new file, when you want to make changes, and so much more. Learning how to use some of these files and what you are able to do with all of the different parts can help you to make sure your code works in the proper manner.

Chapter 5: A Look at the Classes

One part of Python that is important and will ensure that your code is going to work the way that you would like is that it has been organized into classes. These classes are going to hold onto all of the information that you have and all of the objects and will ensure that everything stays in place and works the way that you would like. Classes and objects are going to be an important part of the Python code that is going to help make sure that all the parts that you write out are going to stay in their assigned spots, and they won't end up moving around and causing problems. With this in mind, let's take a closer look at what these classes are and even how you can create some of your own.

These classes are basically going to be containers that hold onto the objects and other parts of the code. You need to name these classes the proper way and put them in the proper spots to get them to work the right way. And you need to store the right objects in your class.

You can store anything that you want inside a class that you design, but you must ensure that things that are similar end up in the same class. The items don't have to be identical to each other, but when someone takes a look at the class that you worked on, they need to be able to see that those objects belong together and make sense to be together.

For example, you don't have to just put cars into the same class, but you could have different vehicles in the same class. You could have items that are considered food. You can even have items that are all the same color. You get some freedom when creating the classes and storing objects in those classes, but when another programmer looks at the code, they should be able to figure out what the objects inside that class are about and those objects should share something in common.

Classes are very important when it comes to writing out your code. These are going to hold onto the various objects that you write in the code and can ensure that everything is stored properly. They will also make it easier for you to call out the different parts of your code when you need them for execution.

Learning how to work with these classes are going to be super important when it comes to working in Python. These classes are going to help hold onto a lot of the different things that you need to work on in this language, will make sure that you are able to pull out the different variables and functions and will make sure that your code doesn't get thrown off and your parts don't get mixed up in the process.

How to create your own class

When you are writing out codes in Python, you have to spend some time learning how to create your own classes because it helps to keep the code organized and ensures that nothing is going to get lost. To make a class though, it is important to use the right keywords before naming the class. You are able to name the class anything that you would like, but you have to make sure that this chosen name is going to show up after the keywords are in place.

After you have taken some time to name a class, you have to go through another step in order to get the subclass named and ready to go. The subclass is the part that will go in the parenthesis. Make sure that when you are done with that first line of creating a class, that you need to have a semicolon in there. While this isn't going to ruin your code if you forget, it is considered the right programming etiquette.

Writing out a class can be pretty simple to work with but it may sound a bit complicated here so we are going to stop here for a moment and look at how you would actually be able to write out this kind of code. Then we will stop for a few minutes and look at the different parts so we can better understand what is going on at any time that we try to create a new class. The code that you will need to make this work includes:

```
class Vehicle(object):
#constructor
def_init_(self, steering, wheels, clutch, breaks, gears):
self._steering = steering
self._wheels = wheels
self._clutch = clutch
self._breaks =breaks
self._gears = gears
#destructor
def_del_(self):
```

```
    print("This is destructor....")

#member functions or methods
def Display_Vehicle(self):
    print('Steering:' , self._steering)
    print('Wheels:', self._wheels)
    print('Clutch:', self._clutch)
    print('Breaks:', self._breaks)
    print('Gears:', self._gears)
#instantiate a vehicle option
myGenericVehicle = Vehicle('Power Steering', 4, 'Super
Clutch', 'Disk Breaks', 5)
myGenericVehicle.Display_Vehicle()
```

The first part of this code is going to be the class definition. This is the part where you will take time to instantiate your object and then make sure the definition for this particular class is in place. This is important because it helps you to stick with the right kind of syntax in your code. Pay special attention to this part of the code that we have because it is the part that will tell the compiler what has to happen here.

Then we move on to the special attributes that the Python code is able to show you. These special attributes are good to use when you need to have a bit more peace of mind that the code is going to work well, and that there isn't going to be a lot of confusion that shows up. If you look through the code syntax that we used above, you should be able to see a few of these, but a few other attributes that can be useful to go along with this include:

__bases__: This is considered a tuple that contains any of the superclasses.

__module__: This is where you are going to find the name of the module and it will also hold your classes.

__name__: This will hold on to the class name.

__doc__: This is where you are going to find the reference string inside the document for your class.

__dict__: This is going to be the variable for the dict. inside the class name.

We then need to be able to assess some of the members of a class. We need to take some time to learn how to do these. You need to make sure that the compiler, along with your text editor, is going to see and then recognize the class that you could create. This is important because it helps them to execute the code in a proper manner. There are a few different methods that are going to help you to make this work when you code, and all of them are going to be good here but our option is going to be the accessor method because it is common and easy to use.

To help us see how this kind of accessor method is going to work, and to understand more of the process of accessing members of your created class better, first take a look at the code below:

```
class Cat(object)
        itsAge = None
        itsWeight = None
        itsName = None
        #set accessor function use to assign values to the
fields or member vars

        def setItsAge(self, itsAge):
        self.itsAge = itsAge

        def setItsWeight(self, itsWeight):
```

```
        self.itsWeight = itsWeight

        def setItsName(self, itsName):
        self.itsName =itsName

        #get accessor function use to return the values
from a field

        def getItsAge(self):
        return self.itsAge
        def getItsWeight(self):
        return self.itsWeight

        def getItsName(self):
        return self.itsName
objFrisky = Cat()
objFrisky.setItsAge(5)
objFrisky.setItsWeight(10)
objFrisky.setItsName("Frisky")
print("Cats Name is:", objFrisky.getItsname())
print("Its age is:", objFrisky.getItsAge())
print("Its weight is:", objFrisky.getItsName())
```

Working with a class is not something that is supposed to be hard to work with. They can help you to take care of all the information that you have and will keep it in order so that it all makes as much sense in the process as possible. You have the ability to create any of the class types that you would like and then add in the objects that you want. Just make sure that the objects that fall into the same class are going to be similar. If someone else takes a look at that class, they understand why an object is found in that class or not.

Both the classes that you create and the objects that you decide to put into them will make a difference in the code and can ensure that it is as organized as possible, will make sure that all of the parts of your code are cleaned up and easy to read, and that they will work together well too.

Chapter 6: Creating your Own Modules

One of the things that you are able to work on when it comes to Python is creating some of your own modules in this kind of library. In this chapter, we are going to spend some time looking at the modules and explaining how the module is going to work. You will find that a module is somewhat similar to a class because it is a collection of the code of Python as well. However, the code in this kind of module is not going to be there to necessarily represent an entity. Instead, we can say that a module is going to be a collection of code that is going to work together in order to meet the same goal.

This kind of definition can seem a bit abstract when you first get started, but it is not that complicated. We have to remember that the modules in Python can contain everything that you need. It could have some functions that be done on their own, along with some classes. In some cases, there are going to be assets that are more static and different in nature including images and so on, though most of the modules that you are going to focus on are just going to be code in Python.

We are able to extend the idea that a module in Python can contain everything. We can use this to say that one module can possibly hold onto another module as well if this is what is going to fit in with the coding that you are doing. This, over time and if it is done enough, is going to result in a structure that looks like a tree. This helps us to see all of the different parts that come with it and how they are going to be connected back together.

Now we need to take a look at what a Python module is all about. As you can probably guess, there is going to be a module for Python that works for pretty much everything. In fact, there are high chances that you can probably solve any problem that is going on in your coding with the help of a module of Python that is existing. Because of this, we want to make sure that we can use the modules of Python that come from other people. This is a simple process to do, can save you a lot of time and effort, and can make coding a bit easier.

To make sure that you are able to use the module that you want in Python inside a code that you are writing, you need to work with the import and the from statements. A few things to note about this to get it to work well will include:

1. The first statement, the *from statement*, is going to be useful because it is going to help you locate the right position in the structure like a tree that comes with the module.

2. Then we move on to the import statement. This one is important because it is going to tell you which of the files of the module you would like to import. Most modules are going to contain a lot of different files, and it is likely that you are not going to need all of this, so specifying which ones you need can be helpful.

Let's say that we want to be able to work with the module that is known as Django, and we want to be able to get the loader file that comes from the template module of there. The code that we would need to use to make this happen will include:

From Django.template import loader

Now, you may find that when working with your Python code, there are going to be a few modules that are already pre-defined and that are installed with Python. However, not all of the modules that are considered Python are going to come with the original download of Python. You may have to go through the manual process of installing the code, as there are too many modules to have them all come originally with Python.

If you are working with a module that has been published officially, then installing it is going to be easy. You can use a little utility that comes with Python called a pip, and if Python is already found on your computer, it should be available on your computer already. If not, you can go through and download from the web to the get-pip.py utility that can help you to install the module that you would like. Once you have had some time to get pip set up, you can then use the install keyword and the name of any module that you would like to install. Let's say that we want to go through and install Django. We would just need to use the small code below to help us get this done.

Pip install Django

You can use the pip in a more advanced manner if you would like as well. For example, you can go through and specify the desired version, set the settings for the proxy, and so on. For most of the programmers though, this usage is going to be plenty. As soon as you have been able to install the module in this manner, it is going to have availability on your Python environment and any application that you want to use will be able to import it.

There are a number of reasons that these Python modules are going to be so popular. They are going to be there to code to scale. In fact, you can go through with a complex kind of application that deals with many problems with the help of this module simply by being able to segment the application so it comes in different and smaller chunks of code. Each chunk of the code is going to be able to help us out with a specific issue, so instead of having to handle the whole application at once, you will be able to take it in smaller applications.

This is going to be nice because it can help to make the development easier. This is because you won't have to worry about the whole picture each time. It is going to add in some more flexibility, especially if you are working with a team of multiple developers. In fact, if your team is larger enough, you can make it so that each of your developers will be able to focus on a different part of the module to get it done.

In addition, if you find that the chunks of code that you are doing are going to get too big, it is possible to take those chunks and segment them out another time into modules. This helps to make sure that any kind of application you are working on is going to be as manageable as possible. On top of all this, the modules are going to be easy to export and install any time that you would like. And the programmer can choose to publish their module in order to allow others to download and install them.

With this in mind, we are going to focus on some of the basics that come with creating modules in Python. The simplest kind of module that you are able to work on within Python is just going to be the simple file, so we are going to focus our attention on that for now. To get started, you need to be able to select a file where you would like to be able to experiment with the modules that you are doing. From this point, you can create two files in it. These files are going to be filbeB.py and fileA.py. Now we are going to start with fileA and add in a sample function to make things easier. The content and the code that we are going to use to make this happen is below:

```
Def sample_function() :
    Print("Hurray")
```

At this point in the game, we are able to import fileA over to fileB and use the sample function that we had earlier. You can write the following code that we have for fileB and then take the time to execute it to see what is going to happen here:

```
Import fileA
```

```
FileA.sample_function()
```

Since we are just using a simple function of sample_function() with what we created in fileA, we can also decide to just import that, rather than doing the whole file. To make this happen, we would just have to change up the code a bit and this would like:

```
From fileA, import sample_function
```

Ssample_function()

In both of these cases, we are going to be using the fileA module. However, we will find that this kind of module is too simple in order to scale to a real application of our choice. You are not going to be able to take this module and export it or install it anywhere you would like. And this is going to only work as long as you have both of the files stay in the same folder. If you move one or the other into a different folder, then working with this is not going to give you the results that you want. As you can imagine, this is not the best structure to use, but it gives us a good introduction to how to create one of your own modules and how you can make this work for your needs.

Working with some of the Python modules can take your coding to a new level along the way. You will find that it is one of the best ways to make sure that the work is going to show up the way that you would like, and that your coding is going to work well.

Chapter 7: The Regular Expressions

We need to take a little detour here and explore a bit what we are able to do with the regular expressions when working in the Python language. One of the things that you are going to enjoy when it comes to the larger library that is in Python is that you can work with something that is known as a regular expression, or an expression that is responsible for handling any kind of task that you would like without all of the glitches, and that are able to handle all of the different searches that you want to do with these.

You will find that working on these regular expressions are going to be good to use in Python because it helps us to go through a large variety of text, including text strings if you would like, and it is possible to use these types of regular expressions to check out the string or the text in your code to double-check whether everything is going to match up in the code in the proper manner or not.

These regular expressions can actually be nice to work with and when you would like to work on one, you can need to stick with the same kind of expression through it, even if you are going to work with another kind of coding language along with Python. Let's say that you are doing some work and you want to code with not only Python but also with other languages like C++ or Java. You would still be able to work with the regular expressions and stick with the syntax that you are familiar with when working on Python.

At this point, we have talked a bit about the regular expressions, but we need to dive in a bit deeper and get more information about it. One of the methods that you can use when it is time to explore these regular expressions is to do a search through the code for a word that you may have spelled out in different ways for your text editor. Maybe you went through and typed out blue in one part, and bleu in another part and you want to get it fixed out, the regular expressions are going to make it easier for you to see it happen.

Any time that you would like to work with some of these regular expressions, it is important to start out by going to the library with Python and then importing the expressions that they have there. You need to do this right now before we start to go much further, or it can be a challenge to do the work later on. Think about all of the different kinds of libraries and extensions that you will need at the beginning of any project and then add these in as well.

There are going to be a few different types of regular expressions that you are going to be able to use when you try to write out some of your own codes. Often, these are going to show up along with the statements, and you must be able to work with them to get the expressions to work the way that you want. To make sure that they work though, we need to spend some time looking at the background and the basics that are going to show up. So, let's get started with learning more about how these regular expressions work.

Basic Patterns

One of the things that a programmer is going to notice when they start with the expressions is that these don't just specify out the character that is fixed that you want to use in the code. In fact, it is possible to bring them out in some cases and use them to find all of the patterns that are going to show up in your code. Some of the different patterns that you need to show up in your statement, as well as in some of the other parts of a Python code, will include:

1. Ordinary characters. These are characters that will match themselves exactly. Be careful with using some of these because they do have special meanings inside of Python. The characters that you will need to watch out for include [], *, ^, $

2. The period—This is going to match any single except the new line symbol of '\n'

3. \w—This is the lowercase w that is going to match the "word" character. This can be a letter, a digit, or an underbar. Keep in mind that this is the

mnemonic and that it is going to match a single word character rather than the whole word.

4. \b—This is the boundary between a non-word and a word.

5. \s—This is going to match a single white space character including the form, form, tab, return, newline, and even space. If you do \S, you are talking about any character that is not a white space.

6. ^ = start, $ = end—These are going to match to the end or the start of your string.

7. \t, \n, \r—These are going to stand for tab, newline, and return.

8. \d—This is the decimal digit for all numbers between 0 and 9. Some of the older regex utilities will not support this so be careful when using it.

9. \ --This is going to inhibit how special the character is. You use this if you are uncertain about whether the character has some special meaning or not to ensure that it is treated just like another character.

One of the ways that you are going to be able to use these regular expressions is to help you complete a query that you would like. There are other tasks, but we are going to focus on the idea of using a query to get things done. The three methods of doing a query with a regular expression that we are going to focus on are the re.findall(), re.search(), and re.match() functions. Let's take a look at what these can do and when we would be able to use these in our code.

First on the list is going to be the search method. To work with this, the syntax is going to include the function of search(). This is the one where you are able to match up things that show up at any location of the string. There aren't going to be some restrictions that you have to worry about when we work on this one, which makes it easier.

With the search method, you get the ability to check whether or not there is some kind of match that is found in the string. Sometimes, there will be a match and sometimes, there won't be based on the query that you make and what is in the code. If there are no matches in that string, then you won't get a result out of this. But if you do the query and the program comes up with a match within the string, no matter where it is found, then the result will be given back. With this one, it is only going to return the information once. There could be ten times the item is listed out, but this one will just show you that it is there, and how many times it is there. The code syntax that you are able to use with this one includes:

```
import re
string = 'apple, orange, mango, orange'
match = re.search(r'orange', string)
print(match.group(0))
```

The second thing that you can do with this is the match method. You can use this option in the same kind of code that we had before, but it is going to go through and look to see if the first word in the sequence is going to match up with your search. If the term is the first word in the sequence, then it is going to show up. If it is not, then you won't be able to get the term that you would like.

In the example above, we would be looking for the orange and seeing if we could find a match that goes with it. But since orange is not listed out as the first word in that sequence, we would not be able to get a match, even though the word orange is present. For this one to work, we need to have it match up right in the first term that is there.

The third thing that we can work with here is the findall method. If you would like to do some work and look at a string, and then get a statement to show up to release all of the possibilities for one word out of the string, then this is the type of method that you would need to use. So, if you would like to use the code above and then figure out how many times the word orange shows up, you would want to work with the findall method instead.

So to keep this one simple and to allow it to work the right way, you would just need to use the syntax that we talked about above and switch out the part with the re.search() over to re.findall(). Then you would get a new result. For this one, since we are looking at orange, we would be able to get the result of "orange, orange" in the end. This is because this method is going to be used to tell us if there are patterns or how many times that a specific word or phrase is going to show up in the code. If you had put the word in five times in the code above, then the findall method would be able to list out the word orange five times as a result.

As you can see, all three of these regular expressions are going to work in a manner that is different in order to help you work on the codes that you want to write. Each of these methods will work in order to help you find the information that you need, look to see whether there is a pattern found in the information, and can help out with so much more. Take some time practicing these to see how they are able to help you get more done in your coding.

Chapter 8: Networking

The next thing that we are going to explore when it comes to working in Python is the idea of networking. This is going to use some of the examples of modules that we talked about earlier and maybe a bit more advanced than we talked about before, but learning how to do this and the different parts that go together can make a big difference when you are creating some kinds of codes in the Python language.

Python is going to provide us with two levels of access to the network services that it has. When you look at the first one, which is known as the low level, you are able to access the basic of the socket support with the help of the operating system on the computer. This is going to be helpful because it allows the programmer to implement clients and servers whether they are working with protocols that are connection-oriented and those that do not have this connection present.

In addition to this low-level option, Python is also going to have some libraries that are considered higher in level. These are going to allow the programmer to have some access to specific application-level network protocols including HTTP and FTP low-level to name a few. In this chapter, we are going to take some of these ideas and explore some of the ways that you are working with Networking Socket Programming.

With this in mind, we need to first take a look at what the sockets are all about and why they will be so important when you work with the idea of networking in Python. Sockets are going to be the endpoints that come with a communication channel that goes bi-directionally. This means that both sides are able to send and receive messages, rather than one side or another being able to only send and the other only being able to receive. Sockets are able to communicate either within the same process, between the processes that happen on the same machine, and even between processes that happen far apart from each other, such as on different continents.

Sockets are going to be interesting and can be helpful with this networking between several processes, and even several different types of machines that you want to work with. You are also able to work with these over a few different types of channels. Some of the examples that you get with this can include UDP, TCP, and the Unix domain. The socket library that you are able to use with the help of Python is going to provide you with a few classes that are designed to handle some of the common transports, along with the generic interface that you can work with and change around in order to handle the rest of the stuff you would like to do.

The neat thing about these sockets is that they are going to have some of their own vocabularies to work with. Knowing some of these terms will make a big difference in how well you are able to work with the sockets, and what you are able to do. Some of the terms that can be helpful when you are working on these sockets and can ensure that your networking with Python will work the way that you want includes:

1. Domain: This is going to be a family of protocols that are used in order to transport the mechanism.

2. Type: The type of communication that will occur between the two endpoints, usually it is going to be SOCK_STREAM for connection-oriented protocols, and then for the connectionless protocols, you would use SOCK_DGRAM.

3. Protocol: This is often going to be zero and it is used in a manner to identify the variant of a protocol within the type and the domain that you are working with.

4. Hostname: This is going to be the identifier that you are going to use with the network interface. Some of the things that we need to know when it comes to the hostname includes:

    a. A string, which can be a hostname, an IPV6 address in a colon notation, a dotted-quad address, or a hostname depending on how it is going to be used in your code.

b. A string "broadcast" is going to tell us what address we are supposed to send the information out to.

c. A zero-length string, which is going to specify the INADDR_ANY

d. An integer, which is going to be interpreted as a binary address in host byte order.

5. Port: And we need to take a look at the term of the port. Each server is going to be set up to listen for the clients calling on at least one port, but sometimes more. A port can be a Fixnum port number, the name of the service, or some other string that will contain the port number inside.

Now, we need to take a look at the socket module and how we are able to create one of these on our own. To create one of these sockets, we need to work with the function of socket.socket(). You will be able to find this inside the socket module, but the syntax that you are going to need to use in order to make this happen includes:

S = socket.socket (socket_family, socket_type, protocol = 0))

At this point, we need to be able to spend some time looking at the parameters and exploring some of the parameters that are going to come with this one. Some of the descriptions of the parameters that we are able to work with will include the following:

1. Socket_family. This one is going to come in as either AF_INET or _AF_UNIX.

2. Socket_type – This is going to come in with the parameters of SOCK_DGRAM or SOCK_STREAM.

3. Protocol: This one is usually going to be the parameter that is left out, and it is going to default to the 0.

Once you have been able to look through the socket object, then you need to make sure that you are using the functions that are required. These functions need to be in place to make sure that either the server or the client program is set up. The functions that you need to make sure that you are including in this kind of module is going to include some of the following for the server:

1. S.bind(): This method is going to make sure that the address, which will include the port number pair and the hostname, over to your chosen socket.

2. S.listen(): This method is going to help us to set up and then start the listener of TCP.

3. S.accept(). This is going to passively accept the TCP client connection and will also wait until the connection arrives, which is known as blocking.

Then we have a few methods that we are able to use that are going to be considered the client socket methods. Some of the different methods that you can use that will work with the client socket methods rather than the server socket methods include:

1. S.connect()> This is going to be the method that is used in order to actively initiate the TCP server connection that we want to use.

Now that we know a bit about the different socket methods that work with both the server and the client parts of the network, it is time to take a look at a few of the general socket methods that can work with both of these. These are going to be pretty simple to work with and can work with both sides based on whether the endpoint is going to accept or send out the message. The different general socket methods that you can choose to use when doing the Python networking will include:

1. S.recv(): This is the method that is going to help receive the message of the TCP.

2. S.send(): This method is going to help to transmit the message with the TCP.

3. S.recvfrom(): This method is going to help us to receive the message of UDP.

4. S.sendto(): This method is going to help us to transmit a message that is UDP.

5. S.close: This is the method that you will use in order to close up the socket that you are working with.

6. Socket.gethostname): This is the method that is going to help return the hostname back to us.

We have spent quite a bit of time taking a look at some of the things that you can do with this kind of programming and some of the terms that you need to know along the way. With all of this in mind, it is time for us to take a look at some of the codes that we can use to make the networking behave the way that we want to in the process.

The first part we are going to look at is creating our own simple server. To help us write out our own internet servers, we have to make sure to use the socket function, which you will be able to find in the socket module, in order to create a new object of a socket. This kind of socket object is then going to be used in order to call up the other functions to ensure that it sets up the socket server in the process here.

Now, we want to be able to call up the function that is known as the bing(hostname, port) in order to tell the program which port you would like to use for the service on the given host. From there, it is time to call up the method *accept* to deal with the returned object. This method is helpful because it is going to wait until the client will be able to connect themselves to the port that is specified. Once this happens, then it is going to return a connection object, which will then be able to represent the connection that you are able to form with that other client to send messages back and forth.

This sounds like a lot, and you may be asking what you would be able to do with all of this. A good code that you can use with Python in order to create a simple server to make the networking do what you want is below:

```
#!/usr/bin/python3          # This is server.py file
import socket

# create a socket object
serversocket = socket.socket(
            socket.AF_INET, socket.SOCK_STREAM)

# get local machine name
host = socket.gethostname()
```

```
port = 9999

# bind to the port
serversocket.bind((host, port))

# queue up to 5 requests
serversocket.listen(5)

while True:
    # establish a connection
    clientsocket,addr = serversocket.accept()

    print("Got a connection from %s" % str(addr))

    msg = 'Thank you for connecting'+ "\r\n"
    clientsocket.send(msg.encode('ascii'))
    clientsocket.close()
```

Now that we have been able to work with the simple server to get the network to behave the way that we want, it is time to work with the simple client. This is going to make sure that the other system is going to be able to handle the information that is coming into you and will make it work so that both parts of the system are going to be able to communicate.

We are now going to spend some time writing out a very simple program for the client, one that will make sure to open up a connection to any port that you would like (we are going to use the port known as 12345), and a given host. This is going to be simple to use because it helps us to create our own socket client with the help of the module function known as a socket.

To start with this one, we are going to use the part of the code known as intosocket.connect(hostname, port). This is going to be useful because it helps to open up a connection that is TCP to the hostname on a port. After you have had a chance to open up the socket, you will then be able to read out from it like with any other IO object. When you are done, you need to remember to close it, just like you would be able to close up another file that you would like to use and that we talked about before.

We need to spend some time looking at an example of how to work with this code. The code that we are going to have listed out below is going to be a client that will be able to connect to our chosen port and host, and will then take the time to read any of the data that is available to it from the socket before exiting when everything is done. The code that you are going to use to make this happen includes:

```
#!/usr/bin/python3          # This is client.py file

import socket

# create a socket object
s = socket.socket(socket.AF_INET,
socket.SOCK_STREAM)

# get local machine name
host = socket.gethostname()

port = 9999

# connection to hostname on the port.
s.connect((host, port))

# Receive no more than 1024 bytes
msg = s.recv(1024)
```

```
s.close()
print (msg.decode('ascii'))
```

Now, once you are all done with this, you want to do a bit of work that can happen in the background. You will need to run the server.py that we have below us in the background, and then we can run the above client.py that we just did in order to get the results that we would like:

```
# Following would start a server in the background.
$ python server.py &
```

```
# Once the server is started, run the client as follows:
$ python client.py
```

Before we stop with this idea, we need to take a look at some of the different internet models that we may run into when we decide to do some of this. A list of some of the modules that are the most important when you are doing some internet programming or some of the Python networks are going to be listed out below.

You can look for these any time that you want to work with a networking internet module. Some of the ones that are the most common that you will see with some of your networking modules that need to be able to work online will include the following:

1. HTTP: These are going to be webpages and are port number 80.

2. NNTP: These are going to be the Usenet news and will be port number 119.

3. FTP: These are going to be the file transfers and the port number is 20.

4. SMTP: These are going to be the ones used for sending an email and will rely on port number 25.

5. POP3: These are responsible for helping fetch emails and will be port number 110.

6. IMAP4: This is another one that you can use to help with fetching email and will rely on port number 143.

7. Telnet: This is going to be the command line and will rely on port number 23.

8. Gopher. This is going to help with the transfers of the document and will rely on port number 70.

Working with networking in Python is a great way to make sure that two processes are going to be able to work together well and will ensure that you are going to see some results with communicating between the two servers or processes, whether they are on the same computer or found on opposite sides of the world from each other. This may be a more advanced method that you are able to use in order to do some coding, but when it comes to coding in Python, you can get it done quickly with some of the results that we just tried out.

Chapter 9: The Process of Multithreading

The next topic that we are going to take a look at when it comes to coding in Python is going to be known as multithreading. This is going to be a type of execution model that is going to allow us to have more than one thread at the same time, within the context of a process. This allows them to share the resources of their process, while still making sure that they can execute independently. A thread is going to be responsible for maintaining a list of information that is relevant to the execution, including the priority schedule, the stack state that is in the address space of the hosting process, a set of registers for the CPU, and the exception handlers for that thing.

Let's take a look at this a bit closer because it may not make much sense right now. Threading is going to be a useful kind of single processor system because it is going to allow the main execution thread so that when the user inputs something, you will see that it is as responsive during the process. Then there is going to be the second kind of worker thread that you are able to execute some of the tasks that are long-running and won't need to have any intervention from the user in the background to get it done.

When you do the process of threading in a system that can handle more than one processor at a time, it is going to result in a true concurrent execution of threads through more than one processor, which is going to make things faster. You have to make sure that you are able to get a system that is strong enough and has enough of the power behind it in order to get this done. If you don't, it is going to run into some trouble because it won't be able to handle both of the threads at the same time.

While the process of doing threading in a multiprocessor system is going to be faster, we have to be aware of the fact that to do this, we need to be careful with the programming. For example, we need to make sure that when we are coding, we avoid any kind of non-intuitive behaviors that show up including deadlocks and racing conditions.

Operating systems are going to be able to use this kind of threading in two main ways. The first one is going to be known as pre-emptive multithreading. This is where the context switch can be controlled with the help of the operating system. The context switching might happen at an inappropriate time. This means that a high priority thread could end up being pre-empted indirectly by one that is low in priority.

Another way that the operating system will choose to work with threading is through the process of cooperative multithreading. This is where the context switching is controlled by the thread. This is going to cause some problems, including deadlocks, if you find that a thread is blocked waiting for the resource to start being free.

The 32 and the 64-bit of Windows is going to work with the first method of multithreading, which the available processor time can be shared in a manner that all of the threads there are able to get an equal time slice, and then they can be serviced based on where they fall in line. During the switching of threads, the context of all the threads that are pre-emptied is going to be stored and then reloaded into the next thread in line. The time slice is going to end up being really short, so short that it seems like the running threads of the process are executing at the same time or one right after the other.

It is easy to confuse the idea of multithreading with multiprogramming and multitasking, which are going to be different kinds of ideas when we are working with the idea of programming and computer work. Multithreading is going to be the ability of a program or a different operating system process in order to manage its use by more than one user at a time. And it is going to manage multiple requests by the same user without having to bring out more than one copy of the program and getting them all to run on the computer.

Each user request that comes into the program or system service (and it is possible here that when it is used properly, the programmer or the user can also be using another program) is going to be kept track of as a thread that has its own identity. As the program works on its job and on behalf of the first request that comes in on that thread, and it is interrupted by other requests, the status of the work on behalf of that kind of thread is going to be kept track of until you are able to get all of the work done.

This is important because it ensures that things are able to run at the same time on the system without running into problems, or any of the work is lost in the process. Even if the first thread has to be interrupted for something more important, the process of multi-threading is going to allow us to work with holding onto the first request and lets it get back to work once the interruption is done. This is a great way to get all of the processes to get the work they want, without having to run the same program a bunch of times to get all of the work done.

Now that we have had some time to look at the basics of multithreading, it is time to take a look at this process when you are working on the Python language. Multitasking, which is a part of multithreading, is going to be the capability of performing more than one task at the same time. But when we look at it in more technical terms, multitasking is going to refer to the ability of your operating system to be able to work on two or more tasks at the same time, without issues with either one.

A good way to think about this is if you are trying to get something to download on your PC while listening to a song and playing a game or even checking your email.

All of these tasks are going to be done on the same operating system at the same time. This is nothing but a form of multitasking which not just helps to save a bit of time but ensures that you are going to be able to increase your own productivity. There are two types of multitasking that you are able to do with your operating system, either process-based or thread-based. We are going to spend some more time looking at the thread-based option.

What is a thread?

A thread is basically going to be just an independent flow of execution that you are able to work with. A single process is able to work with more than one thread at a time, and then each of these threads is set up in order to handle a particular task in the program. Let's say that you are playing a game. The game, as a whole, is going to be just one process but there are going to be several different kinds of threads that are going to be able to help play the music, takes in some input from the user, running the opponent at the same time, and so on. All of these threads are going to be responsible for carrying out the variety of tasks in the same program, and at the same time, without issues.

Every process is going to be set up in a manner that has one thread always running. This one is going to be known as the main thread. This main thread is then going to be the part that can help to create the child thread objects. The child thread is also going to be the part that the main thread can initiate. We will learn in a bit how we are able to check the currently running thread to use it the way that we would like.

When can I use multithreading in Python?

The next thing that we need to take a look at is how to use the process of multithreading when we work in Python. This is going to be a process that is useful when we would like to save some time, while also seeing an improvement in the performance. But it is important to know that we are not able to apply it to everyone.

Looking back to our example of how to work with a game, the music thread is going to be set up in a way that makes it independent of the thread that takes in your input, and the input that it gets from your opponent in the game. If these were not separated out, you will be able to play the game, but it is likely that things would interrupt each other and not work. These threads need to be able to run in an independent manner. This means that you can only work with this process when the dependency between the individual threads is not there at all.

This brings us to the next point of how to achieve this type of multithreading when you work in the Python language. This can be achieved when you take some time to import your threading module. Before you import this specific module though, you need to make sure that it is installed. This is pretty easy when you work with the anaconda environment, and you would just need to use the following code in your prompt to get it done:

Conda install -c conda-forge tbb

After you have been able to go through and install this program, it is now time to import the module for threading so that you are actually able to do the process. The module for threading is simple to use, and the coding that you can use to make it happen includes:

Import threading

From threading import *

Now that you have been able to install your threading module, it is time to move ahead and do a bit of this process with the Python language. First, though, we need to learn how to create some of these threads in this language. There are three methods that you are able to use to make this happen and you have to choose the method that makes the most sense for what you want to accomplish along the way. The three main ways that you are able to create these threads in the Python language include:

1. Without going through the process of creating your own class to go along with it.

2. By extending out the Thread class that you have.

3. Without going through and extending the Thread class that you have.

Let's take a look at how each of these is going to work. The first method is that you create some of these threads without having a class present at all. It is possible to do the multithreading in Python without having to create a class at all, even though it may seem like it is best to work with a class for this. We will look later at some of the methods that you are able to use to add in a class to this, but for now, we are going to look at how to do it without this class. A good example of how you would be able to do this is below:

```
from threading import *
print(current_thread().getName())
def mt():
    print("Child Thread")
child=Thread(target=mt)
child.start()
print("Executing thread name
:",current_thread().getName())
```

Try putting this into your compiler and see what is going to happen with that code. The output is going to show us that the very first thread that we want to use is present, and this is going to be our main thread. Remember that the main thread is important because it is also going to create any of the child threads that you need, the child ones that can execute the function and then the final print statement is going to be executed out with that main thread from before.

From here, we are then able to work with the method of extending out your Thread class in order to handle some of the different things in multithreading. This one is going to be a bit different, but it is going to really help you to get things done. When you have a child class that has been created with your Tread class that has been extending, the child class is then going to be able to represent that a new thread is executing some task or another. When you choose to extend out this specific class, then it is true that the child class is set up to override just two methods ad nothing more. These two methods are going to include the run() method and the __init__() method. With this option, you are not going to be able to override any other methods.

To help you to learn how to extend the Thread class in order to create a thread, you can use the following code to help you get it done:

```
import threading
import time
class mythread(threading.Thread):
    def run(self):
        for x in range(7):
        print("Hi from child")
```

```
a = mythread()
a.start()
a.join()
print("Bye from",current_thread().getName())
```

Take some time to put this into your compiler and figure out what the output is going to do. When you do this, you will find that it is able to show a class that the myclass is able to inherit in the Thread class and the child class. This means that the myclass is going to use the run method overriding for them. By default, the first parameter that comes with this kind of class function needs to be self, because this is going to be the pointer that goes to the current object.

Another thing to consider is that the output is going to show how our child thread is going to execute the run() method and the main thread is going to wait until the execution of the child is all the way complete. This is because the joint() function is there, which is going to tell the main thread that it has to wait its turn so that the child thread is able to finish before moving on.

This method is the one that is usually preferred when you create a thread. This is because it is seen as the standard method. But if you would like to be able to create a thread with the other method that we talked about or you can decide to create threads without extending the Thread class that you are working on and even help with inheriting. We can take a look at how to create one of these threads without having to extend out the thread class, and we can use the code below to help get this done:

```
from threading import *
class ex:
def myfunc(self): #self necessary as the first parameter
in a class func
    for x in range(7):
        print("Child")
myobj=ex()
thread1=Thread(target=myobj.myfunc)
thread1.start()
thread1.join()
print("done")
```

Take some time to add this into your compiler in order to figure out what is going to happen, and to see how this kind of threading is going to happen. The child thread in this one is going to execute what is known as the myfunc, after which the main thread is able to go through and execute what is there in the last of the print statements.

With all of this discussion, it is important to take a look at some of the advantages that come with using threading. Why would a programmer want to take some time to learn how to do this, and make sure that more than one thread is going ton at the same time, rather than doing some of the traditional coding that we can show here? There are a lot of benefits that come with using this threading process including:

1. It helps us to get better utilization of any resources that we have to use.

2. It can help to simplify the code that you are writing.

3. It is going to make sure that there can be parallel and concurrent occurrences of the tasks that you have.

4. It is going to help you to reduce the amount of time consumption or response time, that is going to increase the performance at the same time.

Working with the process of multithreading or threading is going to make a big difference when it comes to the kind of programming that you are going to be able to work with. You will find that there are a lot of important codes that you want to do, and the threads will make sure that it is going to work hard on letting more than one part going on at the same time. Use some of the codings above, and the information that we have about threading to figure out whether these are going to be the right thing to add in with your coding.

Chapter 10: The Database Access with Python

There are times when you are going to want to work with Python in order to access a database and to get through all of the information that is found inside of it. There are a lot of databases that are needed in order to make sure our information is put in the right place, that you can keep track of all the information, and so much more. Learning how to bring Python into the database, no matter what you are doing with it, can make a big difference in the results that you are able to get.

The Python standard that is used when being with a database will be Python DB-API. Most of the interfaces that are used with Python databases are going to adhere to this kind of standard so it needs to be something that you should learn about. You can always choose the database for the application that you are working on. Python Database API is going to support a lot of different database servers, which makes it easier for you to pick the one that you would like to use. Some of the options that work well for this include:

1. GadFly

2. mySQL

3. Sybase

4. Oracle

5. Interbase

6. Informix

7. Microsoft SQL Server 2000

8. PostgreSQL

9. MySQL

Keep in mind here that you need to go through and download out a separate DB API module for each of the databases that you should access. So if you need to change the API that you are working with, then you will need to list out a different module to make it work. For example, if you need to go through and work with both the MySQL database and the Oracle database, you need to download both modules for both of these.

You will find that the DB API is going to provide a minimum standard for working with database in Python and you have to work with the Python syntax and structures when it is possible. The API is going to include a few different things that can help you to get the work done including:

1. It can import the API module that you want to work with.

2. It can help to acquire a connection over to the database that you want to work with.

3. It can help to issue the statements in SQL and the stored procedures.

4. It can help to close out the connection.

Handling some of the errors

There are going to be times when your database access with Python is not going to go as well as you would hope. There are a lot of sources for these errors and knowing what they all mean can be important. Some of the different errors that can show up in this kind of work could be when you call the fetch method for a statement handle that is finished or canceled, a connection failure, an executed SQL statement that has a syntax error, and more. There are a few different types of exceptions that you can handle when doing a database, and some of the most common ones that you are most likely going to see, and their meanings, will include:

1. Warning: This one is going to be used for issues that are going to be non-fatal. It is going to be with the subclass of the StandardError.

2. Error: This is going to be the base class that comes up with most of the errors that show up in the code.

3. InterfaceError: This one is going to be used when there are some errors that show up in the module for the database, rather than in the database on its own.

4. DatabaseError: This one is going to be used when the error that you are dealing with is going to show up in the actual database.

5. DataError: This is going to be one of the subclasses that you are going to see with the DatabaseError and it is going to tell you that some of your data has an error.

6. OperationalERror: This is going to be another part of the subclass of a DatabaseError that will refer

to any of the errors that can be outside of the control of Python

and the programmer who is using it. It could include something like losing the connection with your database.

7. IntegrityError: This is going to be another subclass that can handle situations that would end up damaging the relationship integrity that shows up in the database, including the uniqueness constraints that you try to use or some of the foreign keys.

8. InternalError: This is going to be part of the DatabaseError and it is going to refer to any of the errors that happen internally in the module of the database. This could include having it so that the cursor is no longer active and useable.

9. ProgrammingError: This is going to be a part that will refer to the errors that are there, such as a bad name for the table, and some of the things

that can be safely blamed on the programmer instead of on something else in the process.

10. NotSupportedErorr: This is going to be a part that is going to show up when you want to call up some kind of functionality that is unsupported.

The scripts that you are able to write out in Python are going to help to handle some of these errors. However, before you try to use any of the exceptions that are able or try to handle any of them, make sure that the MySQLdb that you are using has the support to handle it. You can go through and read the specifications to figure out if you are able to do this or not.

Chapter 11: What Can I Do with GUI Programming?

The next topic that we are going to spend some time on is the idea of the GUI or graphical user interface. This is one of the methods that you can use for programming, and Python is going to help us to get it all done. This kind of interface is going to have a bunch of interactive components, including icons and other graphical objects that can make sure that a user can interact with any kind of computer software that you would like, including the operating system on the computer.

The GUI is a useful tool to learn about because it is considered one of the most user-friendly out of all the others, rather than using a command-line interface that is based on text, including the shell that we find with the Unix operating systems, or MS-DOS. You can think about this as the little icons on your computer. If you spend your time just clicking on icons to open up things on your computer rather than opening up a command line and typing in a code to get things done, then you are working with the GUI programming.

The GUI system was first developed by Douglas Engelbart, Alan Kay, and other researchers at Xerox PARC in 1981. Later, Apple started to introduce the Lisa computer that had this GUI in it in 1983. Let's take a look at some of the different things that we need to know when it comes to GUI programming and will be able to help understand how this is going to work better and why we need to work with this kind of interface.

To start with this, we need to take a look at how the GUI works. This is going to use a lot of different options including menus, icons, and windows in order to help you to carry out the different commands that come up. There are a lot of commands that you are able to use with this kind of interface, including moving, deleting, and opening the files. Although this kind of operating system is going to be used in most cases with a mouse, you can also work with the keyboard to make this happen with the arrow keys or some of the shortcuts on the keyboard that are there.

Let's look at an example that comes with this. If you would like to use the GUI system in order to open up a program, you would need to take the mouse pointer and move it the icon for the program that you want. And then just double click from there and the computer will know the work that you want it to do. Your program will work and can help you to open up the program and use it for your needs.

There are a lot of benefits to working with this GUI programming, especially when you are the user of a computer. Most people do not know enough about coding in order to open up the command line and get the right program to work for them. This makes it hard for them to navigate around a computer they want to use. But with GUI, this problem is going to be solved and can help anyone to use a computer, just by recognizing which icon they need to click on to get what they want out of everything on the computer.

Unlike some of the operating systems that are going to use the command line, known as CUI, which is found with the MS-DOS and Unix systems. GUI operating systems can be a lot easier to learn and a lot easier to use because you don't have to know and memorize the different commands that are available. In addition, you will be able to use this kind of system without needing to know how to use any kind of programming language at all.

This is something that a lot of computer users are going to like. The GUI is going to make it easier to use the computer, even if your use of computers and your knowledge of how to run a coding language is limited, then the GUI system is going to be the right one for you to use. Because of the ease of use that comes with this kind of system, and the appearance that is more widely accepted and modern, these systems are pretty much dominating the market for computers and coding that are out there.

Most of the modern operating systems that you want to use are going to work with the idea of GUI. Windows computers, most of the newer Apple computers, Chrome OS, and a lot of the variants of Linux will rely on this as well. And there are going to be a lot of examples that we are looking at that will work with the GUI interface including Firefox, Chrome, Internet Explorer, any of the programs with Microsoft, KDE, and GNOME.

The next question that you may have is how a user is going to be able to interact with the GUI. Most of the time, it is going to be doable with a mouse to interact with almost all of the aspects of the GUI. In some of the more modern devices, especially with mobile, it is possible to use a touchscreen to get it done. It is also possible, in some cases, to work with a keyboard, but most people are going to rely on either the mouse or the touchscreen in order to pick out what they want to do on their computer.

Users who are not familiar with GUI or GLI may want to learn a bit more about these and how they are going to work and how each is different. Even though we are used to working with the GUI because it just includes clicking on the icon on your screen and the information will open up and be ready for you to use, there are times when working with the command line can be the better option, especially based on the kind of project you want to work with. Let's take a look at some of the comparison that you can see between GUI and CLI and how you would be able to benefit from each one.

Topic	CLI	GUI
Ease of Use	Because there is going to be more memorization and the familiarity that is needed to operate and navigate on this system, many new users are going to find that it is harder to work with the CLI than it is the GUI.	Because this kind of interface is intuitive visually, many users find that it is faster and easier to work with the GUI rather than the CLI.
Control	Users are going to have a lot of control when it comes to the operating system and the file in the CLI. However, for someone who is	The GUI is going to offer a lot of access to the files, the operating system, and the software features as a whole. This method is going

	new and hasn't used this method, it is not going to be as friendly for users.	to be seen as more user-friendly than the command line option and it is going to be used more often than the CLI.
Multitasking	Although many of the environments for command line are capable of multitasking, they are not going to offer us with the same kind of easy and ability in order to see more than one thing on the same screen.	GUI users are going to be able to work with a window that helps the users to toggle, manipulate, control, and view through more than one program and folder at the same time.
Speed	The users of the command line will only have to rely on their keyboard	While GUIs are often efficient and fast, they are going to require

	in order to navigate around the interface, which gives them some faster performance in the process.	the use of the mouse. This is going to be a bit slower than what we are going to see with the CLI.
Resources	For the CLI, a computer that is only going to use the command line takes less time and less of the resources of the computer compared to the GUI.	The GUI is going to take more system resources because of the elements that have been shown with loading, including the fonts and icons. Things like video and mouse need to be loaded up, taking up additional resources on the system.
Scripting	A command-line interface is mostly	Creating a script with the GUI is

	going to require the users to already know a bunch of different commands for scripting and the syntax that comes with it. This can make it hard for a new or a novice user to create some scripts.	easier thanks to some of the modern programming software. This is going to make it easier to write the scripts without having to know all of the syntax ad the commands. This software is also going to provide guides and tips for how to code some of the functions that you need.
Remote access	When you use CLI to access another device or computer on the same network,	You will find that this interface makes it easier to remotely access another server or

	the user is going to be able to use this interface in order to manipulate the device and any files. You do need to know how to do all of this and which commands to use so it is harder for a beginner.	computer, and it is easy to navigate, even when you don't have a lot of experience. IT professionals like to work with GUI for some remote access that they need, including the management of user computers and servers.
Diversity	After you have been able to learn how to properly work with the command line, there is not much that will change with it. The new commands can be introduced to this	Each GUI is going to have a different design and a different structure when you want to perform different tasks. Even when you have an iteration of the same GUI, it is

	on occasion but the original commands are going to stay the same over time.	possible that there are a lot of changes with all of the versions.
Strain	The CLI is going to be pretty basic and this can be the cause of more strain on the user's vision. Using the keyboard is not that preferable to a lot of users either. You have to watch your posture and pay attention to how you are using the wrists and fingers in the right manner.	The use of things like shortcut keys and more frequent movement of hand positions due to switching between the mouse and the keyboard, which can reduce the strain that comes with using it. Visual strain can still be something of a risk, but there are more colors with GUI and it is more

		appealing visually so this issue is not as big as it can be with the CLI.

Working with the GUI is definitely something that we are familiar with on most of the computers that we use. Unless you are planning on getting a computer that can just help you to create a program or do coding with, you will find that the GUI is going to be present on the computer. This makes life easier for a lot of users because they just have to go through and click on the icon that they want to use, and they are taken right there.

This has been done in order to cut out some of the work that is needed to reach the different parts that come with the computer and to open up the software and the applications that you have there. This may take out some of the codings that you need to do, but it does make it easier for those who don't know how to code on their own, and who don't have any experience with coding, get things done in the process.

Think about the last computer that you worked on and how it looked. When you started it up, did it have a lot of little icons for the Internet of choice, for Word, and for the other documents and programs that you wanted to use? Or did it have a command line show up and you were expected to type in some kind of code in order to open up any application on the computer? If your computer has some of the first part present, then this is a sign that you are working with the GUI, but if you see the second one, you are working with the CLI.

Both of these have some positives and negatives to work with, but knowing how they work, what you are able to do with each of them, and having a better understanding of when you would want to use each of them is going to be pivotal when you are working on your own coding.

If you would like to do more with coding, rather than relying on the GUI and the graphs that are there, you may want to work with the CLI option so that you are able to write out some of the different parts that come with your own coding as well. But you can definitely work with the idea of the GUI if you find that this is easier to work with and will meet your needs in this process as well.

Chapter 12: What is Machine Learning?

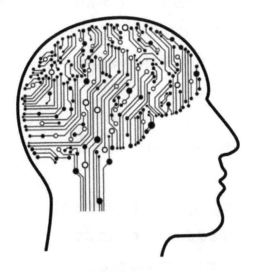

The final topic that we are going to explore in this guidebook is concerning the idea of machine learning. This is a big part of the world around us today and has changed up the world that we see when it comes to programming and coding. In fact, many of the programs that you use on a daily basis, from the search engines to look up things to voice recognition on your phone, are going to rely on machine learning and artificial intelligence to make sure that the code is able to do what the programmer would like.

It is hard for a programmer to be able to come up with all of the things that someone may lookup in a search engine or guess all of the words and phrases that someone would want to use with voice recognition or even all of the different speech patterns. Using traditional coding would make these kinds of things, and a lot of the other options out there, almost impossible. And yet, they are all a natural part of our day. And this is all possible thanks to machine learning.

Machine learning is basically a method of programming that helps the machine learn on its own. This may sound strange, but the program is set up in order to learn from the input and the responses that the user gives to any output that it uses, and then can learn how to give better results over time. This makes it easier to do some of the different processes that are so common today, even when you are not working with a traditional type of code.

There are a lot of different methods that go with machine learning, and these all are going to make sure that we are able to get the right programs done that we would like. It is also possible to add a lot of different coding languages that you are able to use as well but Python is often the one chooses because it is easy while containing all of the power that we need to make the language work the way that we want.

There are three main types of machine learning that you are going to be able to work with, and the choice you make will depend on how much work needs to go into the process you are doing, and what kind of learning makes sense for your chosen project. Each of these is found in some of the technologies that use machine learning right now, so knowing how this works and what you are able to do with it will make a big difference.

With machine learning, you are teaching the computer or the program to use its own experiences with the user in the past in order to perform better in the future. An example of this would be a program that can help with spam email filtering. There are a few methods that can work in this instance, but the easiest one would be to teach the computer how to categorize, memorize, and then identify all the emails in your inbox that you label as spam when they enter your email. Then, if some new emails come in later that match what is already on your email list, the program would be able to mark these as spam without any work on your part.

While this kind of memorization method is the easiest technique to program and work with, there are still some things that will be lacking with it. First of all, you are missing out on the inductive reasoning in the program, which needs to be there for efficient learning. As a programmer, it is much better to go through and program the computer so that it can learn how to discern the message types that come in and that are spam, rather than trying to get the program to memorize the information.

To keep this process simple, you would program your computer to scan any email that is in the spam folder or already known to be spam. From the scan, your program is going to recognize some phrases and words that appear and are common in these spam messages. The program could then scan through any new emails that you get and if an email matches up quite a bit, then it gets automatically sent to the spam folder.

This is a better method to use. But you do need to watch this one a bit. You must pay attention to what is happening during machine learning and realize that sometimes the program may get it wrong. People would be able to look at these emails and use some common sense to figure out if something is spam or not, but the program can't do this.

This can result in some normal emails going to your spam folder. The programmer would need to be able to catch the mistakes and work to show the computer program how it can avoid these issues later on in the future.

There are a lot of benefits that are going to come from implementing some machine learning in the work that you do, and you will find that it is one of the most useful processes that you are able to use in order to get things done, and to ensure the programming is going to do what you want.

Working with Python and machine learning is even better, but no matter which kind of programming language you would like to add to machine learning, machine learning is going to be able to help you in so many ways.

Machine learning can help out by taking some of the complicated tasks that you want to work with and then making them easier. Some of the tasks that you are able to explore with machine learning are going to be too complex in order to do on your own with traditional forms of coding. There may be a few of the options that you can rely on with regular coding, but they are bulky and long and hard to work with. Adding in some machine learning will make this easier and will ensure that you are going to get codes that can take on a lot of work, without as much coding language along the way.

Machine learning is going to be able to help with some of the tasks that are adaptively generated and may not work well with the changes and more that come with working with traditional coding. You will find that conventional programs can do a lot of really cool things, but there are some limitations to watch out for. One of these limitations is that these conventional programs are a little bit rigid. Once you write out the code and implement it, the codes are going to stay the same all the time. These codes will do the same thing over and over unless the programmer changes the code, but they can't learn and adapt.

There will be times when you are working on a program that you want to act in a different manner or react to an input that it receives. Working with a conventional program will not allow this to happen. But working with machine learning allows you to work with a method that teaches the program how to change. Spam detection in your email showed a good example of how this can work.

As we are going through all of this, you may think that working with machine learning is going to be too hard to work with. You may think that it is not going to be able to provide you with the results without having to spend years learning how to work with it and learn some of the algorithms. But in reality, there are many programmers who find that working with machine learning is actually pretty easy. Sure it takes a bit longer to learn, and you need to adapt to some of the different learning algorithms based on what kind of project you are focusing on, but it can really make a difference in the kind of coding that you decide to do and can help you create some cool projects in no time.

As you work through machine learning, you will start to notice that there are a variety of algorithms that work here. These algorithms are going to handle the data that you provide to them in different manners, and the type of data, as well as the information that you would like to get off that information, will often determine which kind of algorithm you would like to use. And the type of project you would like to use will determine the algorithm as well. For example, the program you need to sort through lots of data to make good business decisions is going to be different than the algorithm that you need to make a search engine or to do speech recognition with.

Let's take a look at some of the things that you are able to do when it comes to machine learning and the different learning algorithms that you can use. First on the list is the supervised machine learning. This one is going to be similar to what we see when students are learning in the class. A teacher is going to spend time showing them a lot of examples so they know what works with that assignment and can make estimates on what isn't going to match up.

Supervised machine learning is going to work in a similar manner. It is going to rely on the idea of the programmer showing a bunch of examples during the coding process. The more samples that can be shown, the more accurate it is going to be. You don't need to show it every example that is under the sun though for a specific instance. Instead, you can spend some time showing examples out of your data set, and then, the program can be released and will be able to compare the knowledge it has to some of the input that it gets from the user. There are times when it will guess wrong and not get the result that is needed. But the longer the algorithm is able to practice and learn, the more accurate it will get.

Then there is a type of machine learning that is considered unsupervised. This one is going to work in a slightly different manner than what we saw with supervised machine learning. With this one, you will not need to spend time showing a lot of examples to the computer in order to get the results that you want. You can let the program learn on its own, based on the feedback it is getting from the outputs it provides.

A good example of this is a search engine. There is no way that the programmer is going to be able to come in and think about all the search terms and the best results that go with it. This can make it impossible to work with supervised machine learning algorithms. But the unsupervised machine learning is going to be able to do this because it can search for the results that it needs, and then, depending on the results that it gets from the user, it is going to be able to make adjustments and get better.

To start, we should look at how the search engine works. The first time that you use a new search engine, the results are not always going to provide you with what you want at the top of the results. But as you make your selections, the search engine will make adjustments and it will start to give you the right results that will match up with what you want.

And then there is reinforcement machine learning. This is going to be similar to what we are able to see with the unsupervised machine learning, but it is going to focus more on the idea of true or false. The program is going to learn based on whether the output they use is true, or if it is false, to the user, and then make the right adjustments that are needed to ensure that it learns and starts to give off the right answers that are needed.

As you can see, there is a lot that you are able to do when it comes to machine learning, and using the Python language is going to make it easier to really make this work for your needs. And with a lot of the future programming that we are going to learn how to do, and even some of the different projects that may seem the best for you later on and now, you will find that machine learning is going to be an important topic to work with. If you are particularly interested in this topic, you can find more detailed information in my book ***Python Machine Learning.***

Conclusion

Thank you for making it through to the end of *Python for Beginners.* Let's hope it was informative and able to provide you with all of the tools you need to achieve your goals whatever they may be.

The next step is to start practicing some of the codings that we spent time in this guidebook. We spent a lot of time exploring the different things that you are able to do with Python and a lot of the different aspects that are going to show up in your own coding adventures. While we may not have gone into as much depth as you would see in other locations, we made sure that we knew what each part was about and explored the actual coding that you would need to do with this.

Many people are scared to get into any type of coding because they think that it will be too hard or that they will never be able to figure it all out. But when they take a look at Python, they see how easy coding can be. That is what this guidebook took some time to look at this, and looked at some of the different codes that you want to write with this kind of coding language. We also took it a bit of the more advanced types of coding that you can do with this language as well, ensuring that you are going to be able to get the results that you would like.

There are a lot of things that you are able to do with the Python language and how you can use it with machine learning. This guidebook is going to take some time to look at all of these aspects so you can do some of the codings in the process. When you are ready to begin your journey with Python, make sure to check out this guidebook to help you get started!

Python Machine Learning

A Crash Course for Beginners to Understand Machine learning, Artificial Intelligence, Neural Networks, and Deep Learning with Scikit-Learn, TensorFlow, and Keras.

by

Josh Hugh Learning

Introduction

The following chapters will discuss a lot of the different parts that we need to know when it is time to start working with the Python language and getting it to work for some of your own machine learning needs. There are many companies that want to work with machine learning in order to help them learn more about their company, their competition, their industry, and their customers. When we collect the right data and combine it with the right machine learning algorithms, we will be able to make this work for our needs

Sometimes, getting started with machine learning is hard, and knowing how to get your own program set up and ready to go will be important. The hardest part is figuring out the algorithms that we are going to spend some time working on along the way. There are really quite a few machine learning algorithms that you are able to work with, and picking the right one often will depend on the different processes that you want to do, the questions that you want the data to answer for you, and even the kind of data that you are trying to work with.

We are going to look at some of the basics that come with the process of machine learning and how to pick out the kind of data that we are able to work with as well. Then we will spend the rest of this guidebook looking at some of the different algorithms that we want to handle in this kind of language, with the help of Python. These will ensure that we are able to take over make sure that our data is handled and that we are actually able to see results with the work that we need to do.

There are many types of algorithms that we are able to explore. Some of the options that we are going to explore in this guidebook will include regressions, linear classification, non-linear, and more. In each of these categories, we are going to spend our time looking at how we can get started with this process, and the types of algorithms that fit into each one, and more. When you are done with this guidebook, you will know what you need about some of the most common machine learning algorithms and how to use them for your own data analysis.

There is so much that we are able to do with the Python language, and learning how to use it to pick out the right machine learning can be important. When you are ready to get started with Python machine learning, make sure to check out this guidebook to help you get started.

There are plenty of books on this subject on the market, thanks again for choosing this one! Every effort was made to ensure it is full of as much useful information as possible, and please enjoy it!

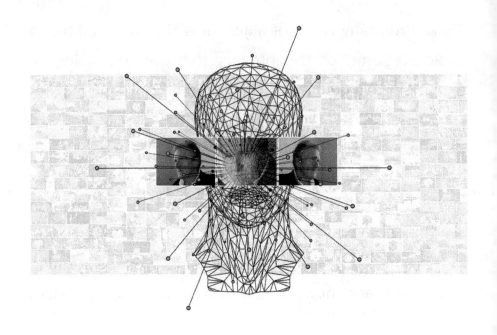

Chapter 1: The Basics of Machine Learning

The first topic that we need to spend some time working on in this guidebook is information on machine learning and what we are able to do with it. This is a huge word in the technology and business world, but many people are not certain about what this all means, and how they are able to work with machine learning to reach some of their own goals along the way.

To start with, we need to take a look at what machine learning is all about and why it is gaining so much popularity in our world today. Machine learning is basically an application of artificial intelligence that is going to provide our systems with the ability to automatically learn and improve from experience, without being programmed on everything that they should be doing. Machine learning focuses on the creation and improvement computer programs that can access data and then use this data to learn.

It all starts with observations, or even data, such as instructions, direct experiences, and examples, in order to look for patterns in data and make better decisions in the future based on the example that we provide. The primary aim is to allow these computers a way to learn without any assistance or intervention from humans automatically, and then you can see that the computer will be able to adjust their actions accordingly to work with this as well.

There are a lot of applications that go with machine learning, and we are going to spend time in this guidebook looking at a lot of the different algorithms and more that you are able to do with machine learning. When you get all of this working together, you will see some amazing results and really see the true potential that comes with machine learning.

There are a lot of different things that you are able to use in machine learning. Any time that you aren't sure how the end result is going to turn up, or you aren't sure what the input of the other person could be, you will find that machine learning can help you get through some of these problems. If you want the computer to be able to go through a long list of options and find patterns or find the right result, then machine learning is going to work the best for you.

Some of the other things that machine learning can help out with include:

1. Voice recognition
2. Facial recognition
3. Search engines. The machine learning program is going to start learning from the answers that the individual provides, or the queries, and will start

to give better answers near the top as time goes on.

4. Recommendations after shopping
5. Going through large amounts of data about finances and customers and making accurate predictions about what the company should do to increase profits and happy customers along the way.

These are just a few of the examples of when you would want to start utilizing a program that needs to be able to act on its own. Many of the traditional programs that you are going to learn how to use as a beginner are going to be much simpler than this. They will tell the computer exactly what it should do in a given situation. This works great for a lot of programs, but for things like artificial intelligence, it is not going to be enough.

In addition, you will find that this machine learning is going to be a really good thing to use when it comes to handling data analysis, which is what some of the algorithms that we will discuss in this guidebook are used for in most cases. There are many algorithms that happen with this, but knowing how to use them and how they fit in with not only machine learning but also data science is going to be important.

Data analysis is going to be really important when it comes to your business and how competitive you can be in the future. You will find that with the right algorithms, and the information that we are going to go through in this guidebook with those algorithms, you will be able to handle some of the different business problems you have, complete your data analysis, and finally gain a good understanding of what all that big data you have been collecting is all about.

The Benefits of Machine Learning

There are actually quite a few benefits that we are going to see when it comes to working with machine learning on a regular basis. This is most likely one of the major reasons why so many companies want to jump on board and see what this is all about. Depending on the kinds of questions that you are looking to answer about your business and more, you will be able to find an application of machine learning in no time.

Machine learning is going to simplify some of the steps that come with product marketing and can assist when you want to make accurate forecasts of sales. Machine learning is going to be able to do this in more than one manner. For example, you will be able to get through a massive amount of data from as many sources as you want. There is likely to be a lot of information in there to help you modify and review all of your marketing strategies until you get the most effective one. You will also find that machine learning can help with rapid analysis, prediction and processing, and it is good at interpreting the past behaviors of your customers.

All of these come together to help you quite a bit, you will be able to use this unlimited amount of information in order to learn more about the customer, figure out what they are looking for in your business, and learn the best way to reach them in the marketing that you do. Considering marketing is an important part of the success of any business, you can easily see why so many companies want to be able to use this for themselves as well.

Machine learning can also help to facilitate accurate diagnoses and predictions in the medical field. This kind of learning is going to help doctors to identify their high-risk patients, make good diagnoses, and give the best medicines that are possible in each case. These are going to be based, for the most part, on available sets of data on patient records that remain anonymous, as well as the symptoms that these patients were experiencing at the time. This can help doctors and other medical professionals become more efficient at the jobs they are doing for us.

When it is time to really work on data entry, but the work is going to take too long to accomplish manually, machine learning is able to step in and help make this happen easier. Data duplication and inaccuracy are going to be big issues for companies who would like to automate the process of data entry. Machine learning can help work with taking those data entry tasks and getting the work done in no time.

Machine learning is also going to have a big impact on the finance sector. Some of the most common benefits of machine learning when it comes to the financial world will include loan underwriting, algorithmic trading, and fraud detection. In addition, this kind of learning is going to help us with continual data assessments to detect and then analyze any of the anomalies that happen in the financial world, which is going to really help to improve the amount of precision that we can find in our models and rules financially.

We will also see that machine learning is able to help with detecting spam. This was actually one of the earliest problems that machine learning was able to come in and help with. Spam filters are able to make up new rules, using neural networks, in order to eliminate spam mail and keep your inbox as clean as possible. The neural network is able to learn how to recognize phishing messages as well as other junk mail when it evaluates the rules that are found across an ever-growing network of computers.

The manufacturing industry is even able to benefit from some of the things that we see with machine learning. Manufacturing firms need to have corrective and preventative maintenance practices in place. However, these are going to be inefficient and costly in many cases. This is where machine learning can step in to help, and it is going to be a great tool in creating a highly efficient predictive maintenance plan that keeps the business up and running and doing well. In fact, when the company follows these plans, it is going to minimize the chances of failures that are not expected to happen, which will reduce unnecessary preventive maintenance activities.

Machine learning is also going to help with better customer segmentation and accurate lifetime value prediction. These are going to be some of the biggest challenges that marketers are going to face on a daily basis. Marketing and sales units are going to have an enormous amount of data sourced from many channels, but accurate predictions are only going to be found when we look at machine learning.

Some of the best marketers out there right now know that they should use machine learning to eliminate some of the guesswork that comes with their marketing efforts. For example, when they use the data representing the patterns of behavior for their users during a trial period, they are going to be able to help their company make predictions on how likely it is to get conversions to a paid trial and figure out if this paid trial is worth their time or not.

And finally, we are able to look at how machine learning is going to be the right option for recommending products and more to customers. This is one of the best ways for a company to cross-sell and up sell to their customers and can be really useful for customers as well. If you have ever gone onto a website and had something like "customers like you bought these products" or something similar, then you have seen machine learning at work in this way.

The models of machine learning are going to analyze the purchase history that they see with the customer, and based on that, they are able to identify the products that the company has that the customer may be interested in. The algorithm is a good one to help us find the hidden patterns among the items and then will group similar products into clusters. This is going to be a good example of unsupervised learning, which we are going to talk about in a moment.

This kind of model is helpful to businesses because it ensures they are able to provide the best product recommendations back to their customers, which is a great way to motivate customers to make another purchase. In this manner, unsupervised machine learning is going to help us to make a really strong recommendation system for the company and can increase the amount they are going to see in profits along the way.

As we can see, there are a lot of benefits that come with working in machine learning, and companies across all industries out there are going to be able to see some of the benefits. Some of the tasks that come with this is making sure that you collect the right kind of data, and that you take your time to pick out a good algorithm that can actually sort through your data and will help you to really hear the predictions and more that you need.

Supervised Machine Learning

Now there are going to be three types of machine learning that we are able to work with when it comes to the algorithm types. We are going to spend some time looking at each one and how it is meant to work overall. Let us look that the supervised form of machine learning. These can apply what has been learned prior and then putting that towards new data, with the help of examples that are labeled in order to predict whether an event is likely to happen in the future or not.

Beginning from the analysis on a known set of data, the algorithm that you choose here is going to be able to produce for us a function to make predictions about the values we are given. The system, when it is working well, is going to be able to provide targets for any new input after you do enough training on it. The learning algorithm is going to compare the output that it gives with the intended and correct output, then it is able to find out any of the errors that are there modify the models in the right manner along the way.

Along with the same kind of idea, but combining some of the work that we will talk about with unsupervised learning later on, includes semi-supervised machine learning algorithms. It is going to work with labeled and unlabeled data to help with the training. In most cases, we are going to see just a small amount of data that is labeled as being used, and then a large amount of data that is unlabeled that is being used. This is because working with labeled data can be expensive, even when it is efficient, and being able to work with this kind of data is going to be hard to handle, and you will need to add in the unlabeled data to get things done.

The systems that are going to work with this kind of algorithm are going to be higher in the amount of accuracy that they will see with their results. In many cases, this kind of learning is going to be chosen any time that the labeled data that we are working with requires skills and relevant resources in order to either train or learn from it. Otherwise, you will find that acquiring the unlabeled resources and data that you need won't require additional work to get it all done.

Unsupervised Machine Learning

Now that we have had a chance to take a look at what the supervised machine learning algorithms are able to do, it is time to take a look at what we are able to do with unsupervised machine learning algorithms. These are going to be the ones that we use any time that the information we have is used to train the algorithm, and it is not going to be labeled or classified. This means that the algorithm, and the system or machine it is on, will need to do the learning on their own, without examples and labeled data to help it make more sense.

Unsupervised learning studies show a system is able to infer a function to describe one of the hidden structures from the unlabeled data. The system doesn't figure out the right output with this one, it is going to explore the data and then draw inferences from the sets of data.

With this one, we are going to use a lot of data that doesn't have a label on it or any information as to the right answer, and then we are able to send it right through the algorithm and let the system learn along the way. This takes more time, and you may end up with some more runs of training and testing before you are done, but it can be one of the best ways to get some strong systems in place to help with your machine learning.

Reinforcement Machine Learning

This is going to be the method of learning that is going to interact with the environment around it by producing actions, and then discovering the rewards or the errors as it goes on. You can compare this one to the idea of trial and error along the way. The trial and error are going to add to the search and delayed reward and are going to be some of the most relevant characteristics of this kind of learning.

When we work with reinforcement machine learning, we are going to find that it allows the software agents and the machine to automatically, on their own, determine the ideal behavior that they should take to maximize the performance that we are seeing. This is something that we are going to call the reinforcement signal.

When we are looking at reinforcement machine learning, there are going to be a lot of similarities to how the computer learns compared to how a human can learn along the way. This method is set up to help us really be able to work with trial and error, and the computer will be able to use this idea to figure out the right course of action to help them be successful. There is so much that we are able to do when it comes to machine learning, and figuring out these different parts, and how to make them work is a challenge that many data scientists are going to have to deal with on a regular basis. When you are ready to explore more about machine learning, and some of the cool things that you as a programmer can do with this language, make sure to read on through below and see all of the different choices in algorithms and more that are available.

Chapter 2: Learning the Data sets of Python

When it comes to working with machine learning and the Python language, there is nothing better than working with data. The more data that you are able to gather and clean, the easier it is to work with some of the algorithms that come with this process. You will find that Python is going to provide us with many algorithms, but we first need to be able to organize the data and get it set up to go through the algorithms for training and testing, in order to see the results that we would like.

With this in mind, we need to take some time to explore the different types of data that we are able to use. We have to look at some of the differences that come up with unstructured and structured data when to use each one, and how we can use these types of data in order to help us train and test some of our Python machine learning algorithms.

Structured Data Sets

The first type of data that we need to spend time working with is structured data. Traditionally we would just have this kind of data in the past, which was harder to get but was easy to work with. Companies would look for some of the structured data that they need, and then make some of the business decisions and more that they need to move forward.

This kind of data is going to be any data that has been organized well and is then going to fit into a formatted repository for us to use. Usually, this is going to be data that is stored in a database so that the elements can be used for more effective processing and analysis.

We may be able to find this kind of data when we are going through other databases to help with the information, or when we get the results of a survey. This one is much easier to work with because it is already organized, and it is going to fit into the algorithm that you want to work with without you have to worry about missing values, duplicates, outliers, or anything else like this. It is also a much more expensive method of working with data, which can make it harder to work with overall as well.

This is why many companies have to make a balancing act over how much-structured data and how much-unstructured data they want to work with. The structured data can make the work easier and will ensure that the algorithm is going to work better, but it is harder to collect, there is less of it, and it is more expensive. The unstructured data is sometimes hard to work with and takes time to clean and organize, but there are endless amounts of it, it can still be used to handle your machine learning algorithms, and it is a lot less expensive to gather up and use.

Unstructured Data Sets

The second type of data that we need to take a look at is the unstructured data. This is basically going to represent any of the data that doesn't provide us with a recognizable structure to it. It is going to be raw and unorganized, and there may not be any rhyme or reason to what you are seeing. Unstructured data is often going to be called loosely structured data in some cases, where the sources of data may have some kind of structure, but not all of the data in that set will end up following the same structure, so you will still have some work to handle to make them work for your needs.

For those businesses that are going to center around the customer, the data that is found in this kind of form can be examined and there is so much that we are able to get out of it, such as using it to enhance the relationship marketing and the customer relationship management that happens as well. The development of unstructured data, as time goes on, is likely to keep growing because more and more businesses are looking to gather this information, and it can be gathered and created in no time at all.

Unstructured data is going to refer to any data that is able to follow a form that is less ordered than items like a database, table, spreadsheets, and other ordered sets of data. In fact, the term data set is going to be a good way to look at this because it is going to be associated with data that is neat and doesn't have any extra content. We are basically working with a lot of data that is not necessarily organized and can be hard to work with without some help organizing.

There are a ton of instances where we are going to see this kind of data. We may see it in documents, social media posts, medical records, books, collaboration software, instant messages, presentations, and Word documents, to name a few. We are able to work with some non-textual unstructured data, and we will see that this can include video files JPEG images and even some MP3 audio files as well.

Most of the data that you are going to work with over time will rely on the idea of unstructured data. There is so much of this kind of data out there to work with, and it is often easier to find and less expensive compared to some of the structured data that we talked about above. Being prepared to handle some of this unstructured data and make sure that it is prepared and ready to go with some of your machine learning algorithms.

How to Manage the Missing Data

We also need to spend some time working with the missing data that comes in. When we are gathering all of that data from all of those different sources, it is likely that at least some of that data is going to come in missing. Whether this is just one part of the data, or there are a lot of values that are missing for entry, we need to know how we can manage these missing data points.

If we tried to push some of these missing data points through the chosen algorithm, it would not end up going all that well. The algorithm may or may not be able to handle some of the issues with the missing data and even if the algorithm is able to handle the missing values, there could be issues with it skewing the results. This is why it is important to choose which method you would like to use when it is time to manage that missing data.

The method you choose will depend on the type and amount of missing data. If you just have a few points that are missing, then it is probably fine to erase those points and not worry about them at all. This can be the easiest method to work with because you will be able to get them gone in no time. However, for the most part, it is important to keep all of the data that you have, and filling them in is a better way to manage the data.

There are a few ways that you are able to fill in the missing data. Usually, going with the average or the mean of the rest of the data, is going to be a good way to start. This ensures that you are still able to use the data that is missing, while not losing out on some of the important parts that you need with that entry as well. Find the standard that you want to use, and then fill in those missing parts so that the data can work better with the algorithm that we are using.

In addition to the missing data, we need to spend some time learning how to manage the outliers and duplicate content. Both of these, if they are not taken care of, is going to skew the results that you get. It is important to figure out the best way to handle both of these before you move on.

To start, we have the outliers. If you have big outliers that are random but really high or really low compared to the rest of the values, you will find that it is going to mess with your results, and those results are not going to be as accurate as you would like. If this is what happens with your data, then it is probably best to just delete the outlier. It is just something that is not that important, and removing it will ensure that you are able to handle the data in an accurate manner.

Now, there are some situations where the outliers are going to be important, as well. If you are looking at some of the outliers, and it looks like there are a number of outliers that are going to fit into one cluster or group, then this may be a sign that we need to move on to looking at these and using the outliers. If you can see that a significant number of outliers are in this group, rather than just one or two random outliers, then this could be a good sign that there is a new option to work with for reaching customers, marketing, the new product you want to release and more. It never hurts to take a look at these outliers, but for many situations, you will want to delete these.

In addition, we need to focus on the duplicates. Many times we will want to go through and delete the duplicates so that the answers don't end up causing any issues with the results that we have. If you have ten of the same person, with all of the same information for them in your set of data, it is going to skew your results.

If this happens a few times, the issue is going to get even worse overall. For the most part, we want to go through and delete these enough so that we just end up with no duplicates or at least a minimal amount of them.

Splitting Your Data

One thing that we will need to work on when it comes to our data is figuring out how to split it up. There is some work that we have to do in order to handle some of the data that we need before we can go through and add them to the algorithms that we want to use. For example, we need to go through a process of training and to test our algorithms to make sure they will work the way that we want. This means that we need to split up the data that we have into the training data and the testing data.

These two sets are important to making sure our algorithms are going to work properly. Having them set up and using these sets in the proper manner will help us to get the best results when it comes to working in machine learning. The rules are pretty simple with this, though, so you will be able to get started without any problems along the way.

For example, we need to make sure that the data we are using is high quality to start with. If you do not have enough data or the data is not high in quality, then your algorithm is going to get trained improperly, and will not work the way that you want. Always be careful about the kind of data that you are using in this process

Next, we need to make sure that we are splitting up the data properly. We should have a group for testing and a group for training. Your training set should be much larger to ensure that you are properly training the data that you have and that the algorithm will get a good dose of the examples that you present and what you want it to do.

Training and Testing Your Data

As we go through some of the processes with working on our data and these algorithms, we have to make sure that we are training and testing all of the algorithms first. You can't just write a few lines of code and then put in your data, hoping to get a good prediction to pop out. You need to take the time to train and test the data through that algorithm, to ensure that the accuracy is there, and to make sure that the algorithm is going to be ready for you to work with.

The first step to this is going to be the training of your data. You have to make sure that you are spending a good deal of time training your data so that it knows the right way to behave. Out of the splitting of the data that we did before; you want to have about 75 to 85 percent of your data be in the training set. This ensures that you have enough data there that will help you to really train the algorithm and gives it plenty of time to learn along the way as well.

Then you can feed all of that training data through your algorithm and let it have some time to form those connections and learn what it is supposed to do. From there, you will then need to test the data that you are working with, as well. This will be the rest of the data that you are working with. You can feed this through the algorithm, and wait to see how much accuracy comes back.

Keep in mind with this one that most of the time; these algorithms are going to be able to learn by experience. This means that while they may not have as high accuracy as you would like in the beginning, they will get better. In fact, you may have to go through and do the training and testing phases a few times in order to increase the accuracy enough that you will use the algorithm to make predictions.

You want to get the accuracy as high as possible. However, if you are noticing that the accuracy tends to be lower, and is going below 50 percent, or is not improving as you do some iterations of the training and testing phases, then this is a bad sign. It shows us that you either are not using enough data in your training for the algorithm to properly learn, or you are using bad data that is confusing the algorithm.

This is why we do the training and testing phases. It helps us to catch some of the problems that may happen with this data and will allow us time to make the necessary changes to the data and algorithm before we rely on the future of our company using badly trained algorithms. We can make the adjustments and run the phases again until the accuracy goes up, and we know that we can rely on that data again.

Working with data is going to be a very big part of working with the machine learning projects that we want to handle, we need to be able to learn how to distinguish the different types of data, how to handle the missing data and the outliers, and how to split up the data so that we are able to properly train and test the algorithms that we want to use. When we are able to work with this, we are going to see some great results through our machine learning, and we will then be able to use these predictions and insights to help improve our business.

Chapter 3: Supervised Learning with Regressions

We spent a bit of time in the first chapter looking at what supervised learning is going to be all about, but we need to spend some time looking at the different algorithms that we are able to work with when it comes to this kind of supervised learning. We are going to start out here with some looks at how to work with supervised learning on regression problems, but then we will move on to those that we are able to do with classification problems later on.

Remember that the supervised learning that we will use here is going to be the kind of learning that provides the algorithm with a lot of examples. The input is going to include the corresponding output so that the machine and the system are then able to take a look at the information and learn what the right answers are. This may seem like it is cheating a bit, but the system is able to learn from those examples and then use that information on some of the unseen and new data that it gets later on.

We can find that this is an effective and quick method of working with machine learning, and it can get our algorithms written out pretty quickly. That is why supervised machine learning is going to be used on a regular basis on these kinds of projects. Some of the different options that you are able to use when it comes to supervised learning with regression problems will include:

The Linear Regression

We now need to take a look at what a linear regression is all about. These models are going to show us, or predict the relationship that will show up between two factors or variables. The factor that we are predicting in this model will be the dependent variable. Then the factors that we are using in order to predict the value of the dependent variable will be known as the independent variable.

Good data is not always going to tell us the full story. The regression analysis is going to be used in research as it is able to establish the correlation between variables. But the correlation is not always going to be the same as causation. Even a line that comes up in a simple linear regression that fits well with the points of data may not be able to say something definitive when it is time to look at the cause and effect relationship that is there.

In a simple linear regression like this one, each of the observations that we have will consist of two values. One value is going to be for the dependent variable, and then the other will be the independent variable. In this model, we are going to work with a straight line that will approximate the relationship between these two.

Multiple regression analysis, though, is when we are going to take at least two, and sometimes more, independent variables, and we will use these in a regression analysis. When this happens, the model is no longer going to be a simple linear one for us to work with.

The linear regression is going to have a number of practical uses along the way. Most applications that come with this are going to fall into one of the following broad categories. The first one is to predict or forecast or for error reduction. This can be used to help with a predictive model when it is time to work with an observed set of data values, and the response that comes. After we are able to create this model, if there are some additional values that are collected without the right response to it, the fitted model that we can use is still able to make a prediction for this.

If we have a goal to use this to help explain variation in the response variable that can be attributed to the variation in the explanatory variable, then this kind of analysis is going to be used to quantify the strength that we are able to see between the response and the explanatory variable.

Often we are going to be able to fit the linear regression with the approach of the least squared, but there are other options to work with based on what you are hoping to get out of the process. The least-squares approach can be used to help fit some models that are not always linear. What this means is that the terms of the linear model and least-squares are linked to one another closely; they are not going to be synonymous with one another.

The Cost Function

A cost function is going to be a mathematical formula that we are able to use to help us chart how something is going to change, especially when we look at production expenses at different output levels. The cost function is able to estimate the total cost that we see in production, given the quantity of the product or service that we are producing.

The management of your company is able to use this kind of model in order to run different production scenarios and to help predict what the total cost would be to produce your product, based on the level of output that you are using. The cost function is going to have its own formula to get things done, and this is going to be $C(x) = FC + V(x)$. Ci is going to be the total cost of production the FC is going to be the total costs that are fixed, V is the variable cost, and then x is going to be the number of units.

Understanding the cost unction of a company is going to be helpful in a lot of different scenarios, but especially when it comes to the process of budgeting because it is going to help your management to understand the cost behavior that we are able to see with a product. This is important to help us anticipate the costs that could be incurred in the next operating period at a planned level of activity. It will also allow the management to evaluate how efficient they were with the production process when the operating period is all done.

We can take a look at how to work with this one as well. Let's say that we are going to work with a toy manufacturer and they have asked to have a cost study to make sure they can improve the budget forecasts for the next year. They pay rent that is $300 a month right now, and their electricity is going to come out to $30. Each toy is going to require $5 in plastic and then $2 in cloth.

With this in mind, we are going to figure out how much it is going to cost for the company to manufacture 1200 toys that year, and then compare it to how much it will cost them to manufacture 1500 toys for the year.

The first thing that we need to do to make this work is to figure out which costs are going to be considered fixed, and which ones are the variable costs. The fixed costs are basically going to be any that are incurred, regardless of how much we are manufacturing the toys, and then the variable will be the ones that we have to pay per unit of production. What this means is that the electricity and the rent are going to be fixed, and then the cloth and the plastic are going to be variable costs.

Let's start out with the steps that we would take in order to produce the 12,000 toys a year. This is going to get us the following equation (keep in mind that the fixed cost here is going to be 330 multiplied by 12 so that we can figure out how much the rent and the utilities will be for the whole year.

C (1200) = $3,960 + 1200(5 + 2)
C (1200) = $12,360

But then we are able to take a look at how much it would take in order to do the same thing with 1500 toys. This one is going to use the formula below to help get it done:

C (1500) = $3,960 + 1500(5 + 2)
C (1500) = $14,460

The fixed costs in this on are going to stay the same, no matter how much output we are going to produce. This is why the cost per unit is going to go down or decrease when we make more units. The rent and the utilities will stay the same regardless of how many units we are trying to produce and sell, so usually working with a larger output here is going to give us more in profits for charging the same amount on the products.

Using Weight Training with Gradient Descent

One of the iterative optimization algorithms that we are going to be able to use when we want to find the minimum of a convex function is going to be the gradient descent. This one is going to be based on ideas of calculus, and it is going to really rely on the properties that happen with the first derivative in order to find out in what direction, and even in what magnitude, the coefficients of our function need to be modified along the way. This gradient descent is going to be used when we have some parameters that we are not able to calculate in an analytical manner, and we need to search for it with an optimization algorithm.

Imagine a large container we would use to eat off of, or a big container that we are able to store some fruit in. For our purposes here, the bowl is going to be the cost function or f. A random part on the container is the cost of the current values of your coefficients. We will see that the bottom then is going to be the cost of the coefficients that have the best set and the minimum of the function.

The goal, when using this process, is to try out more than one value for the coefficients, and then evaluate their cost. This will then allow you to go through and select out new coefficients that you can use, ones that have a slightly lower or better cost than the one you were looking at. If you are able to go through and repeat this process enough times, it is going to help us reach the bottom of the container, and then we will know the values of the coefficients that will give us that minimum cost.

There are a few different types of gradient descents that we are able to work with here. The first one is going to be the batch gradient descent for machine learning. The goal of your supervised machine learning is going to be to estimate a target function that is able to map out the input data over to the output variables. This is going to describe all of the regression and classification problems. This is a good look at what the batch gradient descent is all about. This is going to actually be one of the most common forms of gradient descent that we will see in machine learning.

200

But then we are going to move on to the stochastic gradient descent that is there. These algorithms are going to be slow when you want to run them on some really large sets of data, because one iteration of this kind of algorithm requires that you have a prediction for each instance in training, it can take you a very long time to do this when you have instances that number in the millions.

In these kinds of situations, you can change how you work with the gradient descent and use the stochastic gradient descent. The procedure of a regular descent is going to run, but the update that we see on the coefficients is going to be performed on each instance of training, rather than at the end of the batch of instances. The first step for this is going to require that the order of our set of data for training is going to be random. By mixing up the order that we are doing with these coefficients, we are able to help harness the random walk and make sure that we don't get stuck or distracted.

The updated procedure that we are able to work with this one is going to be the same as the regular gradient descent, but it will not sum out the cost over all of the training patterns. Instead, it is going to be calculated for one training pattern. The learning is going to be faster with this option when we focus on large sets of data.

Polynomial Regression

And finally, we need to take a look at something that is known as the polynomial regression. When we are working with statistics, this kind of regression is going to be one of the analyses of regression that we can work with that will be able to check out the relationship between the dependent and the independent variable and is going to model this relationship as the nth degree polynomial in x. This is going to fit us into a nonlinear relationship between the value that we see with x and the corresponding conditional mean of y.

There are a lot of times when we will use this kind of regression, especially when we want to work with something like the growth rate of tissues, the distribution that we are able to find with carbon isotopes in some of the lake sediments that we see, and the progression of disease epidemics.

Although this regression is going to take some of our nonlinear models and has the data fit it, it is going to be more of a statistical estimation problem. It is going to be linear with the idea that the regression function is going to be linear in some of the unknown parameters that we have with the estimated data. For this reason, it is going to be considered one of the cases of multiple linear regressions.

The independent variables that show up are going to result from the polynomial expansion of the baseline variables, and they are going to be known as higher-degree terms. Such variables can be used when we are doing settings of classification.

There would be times that we would be working with regression problems when it comes to working with machine learning. Adding in some of these regression algorithms can help you to sort through the data that you have in a more efficient manner, and will ensure that you are able to get your data sorted through and find out the predictions and insights that you are looking for as well. Some of the other times when we would want to work with the polynomial regression will include:

1. When the researcher thinks that there are some relationships that will fit on a curved line. Clearly, these types of cases are going to show us a term that is polynomial.

2. When we want to do an inspection of the residuals, if we try to fit a linear model to a data that is curved, then the scatter plot of residuals on the predictor is going to have patches of many positive residuals in the manner. If this does happen, then we can see that this kind of situation is not going to be appropriate for the needs that we have.

3. An assumption in the usual multiple linear regression analysis that all of our variables that should be independent are actually this way. in this kind of model, we will find that this is an assumption that is not going to be satisfied at all.

Basically, we will find that the biggest goal of this kind of analysis of regression is that we want to model the expected value that is going to show up in our dependent variables. We would do this in terms of the value of our independent variable that is going to be x. This will help us to get some of the work that we need to be done when it comes to this kind of regression as well.

Chapter 4: Regularization

To start here, we need to look at some of the foundations of overfitting. Let's assume that you are looking to make some predictions on the price movement of a stock in the future. We then decide to go through and gather up some of the historical daily prices of the stock, maybe going back over the past ten days or so, and then plot the stock price on a scatter plot as we would need. You would then want to go through and capture some of the information about the movements of the stock price. You are then able to assess and gather data for 16 features that you would like to follow because you know the stock price is going to be dependent on them. These are going to include:

1. The competition of the company.
2. The sentiment of the investors
3. The Foreign Exchange Rates
4. The interest rates
5. Inflation rate
6. The future contracts of the company.
7. The current contracts of the company
8. Information on the management of the company
9. The state of the M&A of the company
10. The current and the size of the futures contract of the company.
11. The dividends that the company is able to provide.
12. Any future announcements that the company may release.
13. The profits that the company is making.
14. The earnings of the company.
15. How the industry as a whole is performing at the time.

Once we have been able to gather, clean, scale, and transform the data, it is time to split it out into training and test sets of data. You will need to go through and feed the training data into the model that you chose for machine learning in order to get it trained. After you have had some time to train the algorithms or the models, you can then go through and test out the accuracy that happens with the model by passing through the set of test data.

The goal with this is actually to go through and chart out the prices. You should find that the actual prices of the stocks are going to be random. However, the predicted price of your stock is going to fall into a smooth curve. It has not gone through and fits itself too closely with the training set that you have, and this helps us to work with the generalization of the unseen data better.

Different Types of Fitting with Predicted Prices

We may want to make sure that we want to assume that the plot actual versus the predicted stock prices and we are going to then come up with a few different types of charts along the way:

1. Straight Line to Show Predicted Price

When we have a chart that shows the predicted price in a straight line, this shows us that the algorithm has gone through and has come up with a really strong pre-conception about the data. This is usually a sign that there is a high bias in the information and will show us something known as underfitting. These are not good models to use when you would like to predict new data and should be thrown out in most cases.

2. A Very Strong Closely Fitted Line

This one is an example of the other possible extreme. It may look like it is doing a really good job helping us to predict the price of the stock. However, this is going to be something that is known as overfitting. This is also going to be seen as a high-variance because it has learned the training data in a manner that is so accurate that it will not be able to generalize the information well. This makes it hard to go through and make some predictions on the new and unseen data that is there. These models are also not going to be good when you want to use them to make predictions on the new data.

If we go through with this model and feed it some new data, then you will find that the accuracy of those predictions is going to be really poor. It is also going to be a sign that we are not providing the model with enough data for training. Overfitting is when the model is going to over train itself on the data that you used for this purpose. This could be because we have too many features showing up in the data or because the algorithm has not had time to go through enough data. It is going to happen when the difference that shows up between the predicted values and the actual values is close to 0.

How to Detect Overfitting

Now that we have taken a look at why this overfitting is such a bad thing, it is important for us to go through and figure out when overfitting is going to occur and then figure out how to fit it. The models that you are working with that have been overfitting on the training data will be the ones that are not able to generalize well to the new examples. These are not going to be very good at predicting some of the data that is not seen yet.

This means that when you are trying to add new data to the mix, then you are going to end up with an algorithm that is not doing its job very well. This implies that the model is going to be extremely accurate during training, but when it is time to make predictions on data that it has not seen before, the results are going to be poor overall.

If the measure of accuracy, such as mean error squared, ends up being quite a bit lower when you are working with training the model, and then you see that the accuracy starts to deteriorate on the set of data that you are using for testing, then this is a good sign that overfitting is happening with the data and you may need to supply it with different data, or at least more data, in order to increase the accuracy again.

Often the best way for us to go through with this and figure out whether or not there is overfitting with the data that we want to use, is to chart out the results on a graph. This may seem like we are getting ahead of ourselves, but these visuals will really help us to see some of the complex relationships that are going to show up on our data, and they can tell us almost instantly whether there is an issue with overfitting going on.

When you are working with a particular algorithm, and you are worried about the issue of overfitting, you simply need to go through and plot out the graph. If there is a straight line that shows up on the graph, and all of the points are right on the line, or at least touching the line that is there, then this is a bad sign that overfitting is going on. It is time to go back through and check on the data that you are using, or maybe just do some more training with a wider variety of data, in order to fix this kind of problem.

How Can I Fix Overfitting?

The good news is that there are a few steps that we are able to work in order to help fix some of the issues that come with overfitting. First, we are able to randomly remove some of the features that we are putting into the algorithm, and then use this to help us assess the accuracy of the algorithm in a more iterative manner. However, this can be effective, but the process is slow and can be really tedious. There are going to be four common methods that we are able to use in order to reduce some of the overfittings that we see. Some of these include:

1. **Reduce the features:** The most obvious out of the options that we are able to use is to reduce some of the features. You are able to compute the correlation matrix of our features, and then we can reduce some of the features that happen to be the most highly correlated with one another.

2. **Model selection algorithms:** Another method that we are able to use is going to be the model selection algorithms. These are the algorithms that have the power to choose the features that have the greatest importance and keeps those around, while limiting some of the others that don't seem to affect the data as much The biggest problem that we are going to see with this one is that it is possible to lose out on some valuable information at times.

3. **Feed-in more data:** We can also take a look at feeding in more data to the model. Sometimes this is all that we need in order to handle some of the issues that come with overfitting. You should aim in training a set to feed in enough data to the models so that you are able to train, test, and validate the model thoroughly. For example, you

should do about 60 percent of your data to help train the model, 20 percent to test the data, and then 20 to help validate the model that you are working with.

We need to explore the idea of regularization a bit more. The aim of this is to help keep all of the features, but then impose a constraint on the magnitude of the coefficients that you are able to get. This is often seen as the preferred method because you do not have to lose out on any of your features because you are busy penalizing them like some of the other methods. When the constraints are applied to the parameters, then the model is going to end up not overfitting as much because it can produce a smooth function.

The parameters that we work within regularization, which are going to be known as the penalty factors, are going to be able to introduce which controls the parameters and will ensure that the model is not going to over train itself on any of the training data that you are working with. We will also find that these parameters are going to be at smaller values to help eliminate the issue of overfitting. When the coefficients work with larger values, then the regularization parameters are going to penalize some of the optimization functions that are there.

While we are on regularization, we should look at the two most common techniques that we are able to work with on this. The first one is going to be Lasso. This is going to be a tool for feature selection, and it is going to be able to help us eliminate any of the features that not important to what we are doing. It can also add in a penalty, which is going to be the absolute of the magnitude that we will see with the coefficient.

What this is going to do is ensure that the features we are working with are not going to end up applying some high weights to the prediction that comes with our algorithm. The result of this is that some of the weights are going to turn into zero. This means that the data of some of our features are not going to be seen as important at all, and they will not be used in the algorithm that we have at all.

And the second technique that works here is going to be a ridge. This one is a bit different but can still have a lot of the features and strengths that we need. With ridge, we are going to add in a penalty, which is going to be the square of the magnitude of the coefficients. As a result of this, you will find that some of the weights that we have are going to end up being close to 0. This is a good way to smooth out some of the effects that we will see on the features as well.

Overfitting our data is something that can be a big issue when we are working with machine learning. We want to get accurate information out of what we are doing in this process, and if the algorithm ends up overfitting, then it is not guessing the data very well. It may do well with the training data that we are working with, but it is not going to do all that well when it comes to taking on new data, and that is when you really need this algorithm to work its best.

Following some of the techniques that we have in this chapter, and learning how this overfitting occurs in the first place, is going to be one of the important first steps that you can follow in order to make sure that this issue doesn't happen - the more that you are able to prevent this from happening, the more accurate and efficient your models will end up being in machine learning. When we can keep underfitting and overfitting from happening with some of the data that we have, we are going to get amazing results, and our models will work in the manner that we want.

Chapter 5: Supervised Learning with Classification

Supervised machine learning is going to be one of the algorithms that you will use a lot in machine learning because there are a lot of applications. This is a good and effective method of teaching your machine on algorithms and how you would like it to behave. This is because this method is going to show the algorithm all of the examples, with their corresponding answers, right from the beginning, making sure that the algorithm is able to learn the right way faster than before.

This is why there are going to be so many different types of supervised machine learning models and algorithms that we are able to work with. They may take a bit more time in the beginning, but when we use classification and some of the other tools that are out there to help us get it all done, we will find that it is easier to train and test out our models and get some good results in the process. Some of the different supervised machine learning algorithms that we are able to focus on with classification will include:

Logistic Regression

The next algorithm on the list that we need to take a look at is going to be the logistic regression. These are going to be able to help us out with a lot of different problems that we want the data to solve, and if we are able to use it in the right manner, we are going to be able to see some amazing results in the process. As time passed, it started to be used for applications in the social sciences. Logistic regression, though, no matter how we decide to work with it, is going to be used when the target, or our dependent variable, is categorical.

This means that we may use it for a few different situations, such as when we would like to predict whether or not an email that comes to us is spam, or whether or not a tumor is malignant.

To help us see how this goes, we can start with a scenario where we would like to determine whether or not an email that we see is spam or not. If we use linear regression for this instance, we would need to set up a basis wherewith to base our classification with.

From this example alone, it is easy to see that the linear regression is going to fail a bit when it comes to some of the classification problems. Linear regression is not going to be bounded, and this is why we need to work with logistic regression for some of our problems. With this one, the value is going to range from 0 to 1, and nothing in between.

Now, we may see that there are a few different types of logistic regression that we are able to work with. The three main types that we are able to focus our attention on here are going to include:

1. The binary logistic regression: This is going to be a response that is categorical and has only two outcomes possible. When we are looking at emails, for example, it is going to tell us whether the specific email is spam or not.

2. Multinomial logistic regression: This is when there are three or more categories that show up without any order. For example, we may see this one when predicting which food is preferred more such as Vegan, Non-Vegan, and Vegan.

3. Ordinal logistic regression: This is when there are at least three categories, bust sometimes more, to the ordering. For example, we could have a movie rating that goes from one to five.

To help make it easier to predict which class our data is going to belong to, we are going to set a threshold in the beginning. Based on what this threshold is about, the obtained estimated probability is going to be classified into classes. Going back to the idea of the spam earlier, we could have our predicted value be at or above 0.5. When an email reaches this threshold, then the email is going to be seen as spam. If it does not, then it is not seen as spam.

The decision boundary that we are able to work with is going to be seen as non-linear or linear. If preferred the Polynomial order can be changed to get to a more varied boundary if we would prefer. This would give us the variation that we would need.

When we work with the logistical regression, we will find that there are a lot of the other parts we have talked about in this guidebook so far that they are going to show up in the code. This is because there are often times when we need to combine together more than one option when it comes to working with these algorithms. A good way to see some of this is to look at an example of the coding that is needed to work on the logistical regression, and we can see that below:

```
def weightInitialization(n_features):
w = np.zeros((1,n_features))
b = 0
return w,bdef sigmoid_activation(result):
final_result = 1/(1+np.exp(-result))
return final_result
def model_optimize(w, b, X, Y):
m = X.shape[0]

#Prediction
final_result = sigmoid_activation(np.dot(w,X.T)+b)
Y_T = Y.T
cost = (-1/m)*(np.sum((Y_T*np.log(final_result)) + ((1-
Y_T)*(np.log(1-final_result)))))
```

```
#

#Gradient calculation
dw = (1/m)*(np.dot(X.T, (final_result-Y.T).T))
db = (1/m)*(np.sum(final_result-Y.T))


grads = {"dw": dw, "db": db}


return grads, costdef model_predict(w, b, X, Y,
learning_rate, no_iterations):
costs = []
for i in range(no_iterations):
#
grads, cost = model_optimize(w,b,X,Y)
#
dw = grads["dw"]
db = grads["db"]
#weight update
w = w - (learning_rate * (dw.T))
b = b - (learning_rate * db)
#


if (i % 100 == 0):
costs.append(cost)
#print("Cost after %i iteration is %f" %(i, cost))
```

```
#final parameters
coeff = {"w": w, "b": b}
gradient = {"dw": dw, "db": db}

return coeff, gradient, costsdef predict(final_pred, m):
y_pred = np.zeros((1,m))
for i in range(final_pred.shape[1]):
if final_pred[0][i] > 0.5:
y_pred[0][i] = 1
return y_pred
```

Many times the logistical regression is going to be a better choice to go with compared to the linear regression. This is because this will allow us to catch some of the instances that are going to be missed, like what is going to happen with the linear regression.

Multiclass Classification

While we are here, we also need to take a look at some of the benefits of working with the multiclass classification. Classification problems are often going to come with many classes, and there is going to be an imbalanced kind of dataset that will present a different challenge compared to what we see with some of the classification problems. Sometimes the skewed distribution is going to make some of the other algorithms with machine learning less effective, especially when it comes to predicting minority class examples.

We will find that with a multiclass classification problem, you are going to be handling a task of classification that has three or more classes to work with. This means that we could do something like classifying a set of images of fruits, which may be things like pears, apples, and oranges, and some other fruits if you would like to add these in as well.

This kind of classification is going to make some assumptions in order to make sure that things are going to happen. For example, it will make one assumption that each of the samples is going to be assigned to one and no more than one label. For example, fruit can be either a pear or an apple, but it is not possible for this fruit to be both at the same time.

While some of the classification algorithms that are out there are naturally going to be set up to permit the use of more than two of these classes, others are going to be binary algorithms instead, and these can also be turned into multinomial classifiers with a lot of different strategies along the way. One thing to remember with this one though is that we should not confuse this kind of classification should not be confused with the idea of multi-label classification, where the multiple labels are to be predicted for each instance.

There are many times when we are going to work with the classification problems, especially when it comes to handling things with supervised machine learning. These can make it easier to split up some of the different algorithms that you have and will ensure that you are able to see what classes are there, and how to understand some of the data that you have available.

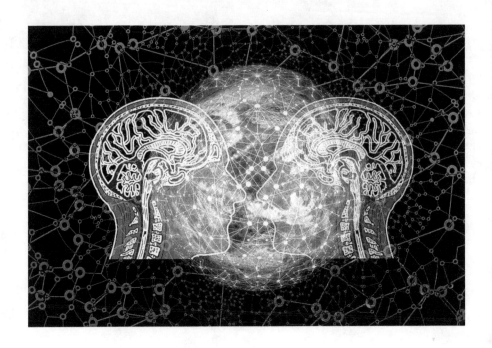

Chapter 6: Non-linear Classification Models

There are a lot of things that we are able to do when it is time to work with some of the classification problems that we have along the way. These are really useful when it is time to work through some of the data that we have, and they can often be one of the best ways that we are able to learn about the data, see which groups the data falls into, and so much more. Some of the other classification models that you are able to work with, the ones that do not fit in with the linear classification models, will include some of the following:

K-Nearest Neighbor

The first option that we are going to look at when it comes to working on the non-linear classification models will include the K-Nearest Neighbor or the KNN algorithm. This is going to be an example of a supervised machine learning algorithm, so we will need to have some labeled data in place as well.

There are a few benefits that you will see when it is time to work with the KNN algorithm. When we are working with the algorithm, it is helpful for us to cut down the noise that may be in the set of data. Depending on the data that we are working with, you may find that the noise is going to be really loud, and making sure the noise is gone going to ensure that we are able to handle the work as well and get more accurate results in the process.

There are many algorithms that we are able to work with when it comes to working with machine learning. This makes it hard to know why you would want to work with this kind of algorithm over some of the others. The benefits of working with the KNN algorithm and why you would want to choose it over some of the other options include:

1. It can work well with problems, even if they are considered multi-class.

2. You are able to apply this algorithm to both problems that are regressive and those that are classification.

3. There aren't any assumptions that come up with the data. This ensures that you get the information that you want, rather than having any assumptions in the place, causing some issues.

4. It is an easy algorithm to work with. It is easy to understand, especially if you are brand new to the machine learning process.

However, there are more options for algorithms that you are able to work with because the KNN algorithm isn't going to be perfect in each and every situation that you go to. Some of the negatives that come with using the KNN algorithm include:

1. It is going to be computationally and memory intensive expensive. If you don't have the right system and the right amount of space to work with, it is going to make it more difficult to see the results that you want from this algorithm.

2. If there are a lot of independent variables that you are going to work with, you will find that the KNN algorithm is going to struggle.

3. The KNN algorithm isn't going to work that well if you have any rare event, or skewed, target variables.

4. Sensitive to the scale of data.

For any of the problems that we are going to work with, you will find that having a smaller value of k is going to give us more variance in any of the predictions that we are working with. In addition, when you set it so that k is at a bigger value, it is possible that there is going to be more bias in the model as you work on it too.

While you are working with this one, though, there may be times when you will need to go through and create some dummy variables. This is going to make it easier to figure out the categorical variables that will show up in this algorithm. This is different than the regressions that we will look for though because you can work with creating the k dummies rather than just the k-1.

With this in mind, we need to take a look at the best way to handle finding these k values in the first place. This is often done with the use of cross-validation. It is going to be important to use this process in order to estimate what the error of validation will be. To make this happen, we will need to hold out a subset of the training set from the process of building up the model.

Cross-validation is going to involve us going through and dividing up our training data randomly. We are going to work with a 10 fold validation, so that means we would want to divide up the training sets that we have into 10 groups. We want to keep them as close to the same in size as possible as we go through the dividing. From this, 90 percent of our data is going to be the kind that we use to train our model. The other ten percent or so will be used to help validate the model that we are working with and to test whether or not it is working.

The misclassification rate that we need to focus on for this one is going to be computed when we look at the ten percent that you saved back for the validation. This procedure is going to need to go through and repeat itself ten times because of how we are doing all of this. Each of the groups of observations that we run into is going to be seen as validation, and then you can test it as well.

Decision Trees and Random Forests

Often, the decision tree and the random forest are going to work together. These are going to be efficient tools of data that will help you to take two of the choices that you would like to work with, especially when the choices are very different, and then will use this information in order to help you pick out which decision is the best for your needs so that you can grow your business and more.

When you are presented with more than one option, and they all look like they are good options to work with, the decision tree is going to be a good option to choose along the way. These will help you to take some of these choices and then see what the possible outcomes may be with these, making it easier to figure out what is the best course of action to take.

Now, you will find that there are a few different ways that you are able to work with these decision trees. Many of those who are working with machine learning will use it if either of their variables is categorical, and one is random. However, there are times when you will need to use these decision trees with some of the classification problems that you have. To ensure that you are picking out and creating your decision tree well, then you need to make sure that you take all of the sets of data that you have and then split them up to be in two or more sets, with some similar data in each one. You can then sort this out with the help of independent variables because it will help you to set it up the way that the decision tree needs.

Sometimes the decision tree is not to be what we need, and we will find that it is better to have more than one decision tree to get the work that we want. This is when the decision tree is going to be turned over to a random forest. These are popular to work with because they allow you to look at many possible, decisions that you want to make, and come up with the one that you would like to work with. So, the best way to think about these random forests is that they are going to be a bunch of different decision trees that are going to work together.

There are going to be many applications of using the random forest. This is because the random forest is perfect most of the time, it is going to do a better job of providing you with some insights and predictions than some of the other algorithms. Some of the ways that you are able to use these forests and make sure that they will benefit you include:

- When you are working on your own training sets, you will find that all of the objects that are inside a set will be generated randomly, and it can be replaced if your random tree things that this is necessary and better for your needs.
- If there are M input variable amounts, then m<M is going to be specified from the beginning, and it will be held as a constant. The reason that this is so important because it means that each tree that you have is randomly picked from their own variable using M.

- The goal of each of your random trees will be to find the split that is the best for the variable m.

- As the tree grows, all of these trees are going to keep getting as big as they possibly can. Remember that these random trees are not going to prune themselves.

- The forest that is created from a random tree can be great because it is much better at predicting certain outcomes. It is able to do this for you because it will take all prediction from each of the trees that you create and then will be able to select the average for regression or the consensus that you get during classification.

Random forests are a good tool that a programmer is able to use when they would like to make sure that they add in some data science to the machine learning that you are doing, and there are going to be many benefits. But any time that you are looking for an easy way to look through some of the options that are available for your work, and you want help making some smart decisions, then the decision trees and random forests will be the best option for you to choose.

Working with Support Vector Machines

We can also spend some time working with the support vector machines, or SVM. These are going to be there to help us take each set of the data and then plot them so that they will show up on one n-dimensional of N. N is going to be the number of features that you would like to work with all of this. You will then be able to take the value of the features and work to translate this over to the value that you will need for your chosen coordinates. The job that you are able to do when it is time to reach this point is to figure out where your hyperplane will fall because this is going to be the part that will show you what differences are there between the classes that show up.

Here you may notice that it is possible that more than one support vector is going to show up. The good news is that many of these are obviously not going to be important, and they are just going to be the coordinates of the individual observations that you are going to see here. Then you are able to work with the SVM to turn into your frontier, the part that is able to separate these parts into classes, and then there will be the line and the hyperplane, which are the two parts that we need to focus on the most.

Up to this point, some of the work that we are looking at will seem a bit confusing. But there are a few steps that we are able to follow in order to really find out how to sort this data and use the SVM for our needs. First, we need to look for our own hyperplane. One thing that you will notice is that this algorithm is going to bring out more than one hyperplane that we can focus on. This is a challenge for beginners because you want to make sure that the hyperplane you pick is going to be the best one for sorting through the data and making it work for your needs.

The good thing to remember here is that even if you do have a few options when it comes to hyperplanes, there are still going to be some easy steps that we are able to use to help us pick out the right one. The specific steps that you are able to use when trying to figure out the hyperplane for your SVM will include:

- We are going to start out with three hyperplanes that we will call 1, 2, and 3. Then we are going to spend time figuring out which hyperplane is right so that we can classify the star and the circle.
- The good news is there is a pretty simple rule that you can follow so that it becomes easier to identify which hyperplane is the right one. The hyperplane that you want to go with will be the one that segregates your classes the best.

- That one was easy to work with, but in the next one, our hyperplanes of 1, 2, and 3 are all going through the classes, and they segregate them in a manner that is similar. For example, all of the lines or these hyperplanes are going to run parallel with each other. From here you may find that it is hard to pick which hyperplane is the right one.

- For the issue that is above, we will need to use what is known as the margin. This is basically the distance that occurs between the hyperplane and the nearest data point from either of the two classes. Then you will be able to get some numbers that can help you out. These numbers may be closer together, but they will point out which hyperplane is going to be the best.

The Neural Networks

We would be working with the Scikit-Learn library in this process of machine learning, and one that can handle a lot of really things for machine learning will be the neural networks. These are used quite a bit because they will work similar to the human brain, picking up on different patterns and more, and forming stronger connections each time that something is correct with its predictions.

When we are working with these neural networks, we will find that there are often a lot of layers, and each of these layers is going to be spending time to see whether there are some patterns there are not. If the network is able to find that new pattern, then they will go on through to the next layer. And this process will continue until there are no more patterns for the process to find, and until we are done and the neural network is able to make some predictions as well.

There are a few things that will happen at this point, based on how the program works. If the algorithm went through the process above and was able to sort through all of the different layers, it will then make a prediction. If that prediction is right, the neurons in the system will turn out stronger than ever. This is because the program has used artificial intelligence in order to make some strong associations between the patterns and the object. The more times that the system can come back with the right answer, the more efficient it will be when you turn it on and use it again.

Now, this may seem a little bit farfetched, but a closer examination of these neural networks will help us to see how they work together and why they are so important. For our example, let's say that your goal is to create a program that is able to take a picture that you input into it, and then, by looking at that picture and going through the layers, the program is able to recognize that the image in that picture is that of a car.

If the program has been set up in the proper manner, it is going to make the right prediction that there is a car in the picture. The program is able to come up with this prediction based on some of the features that it already knows belongs to the car, including the color, the number on the license plate, the placement of the doors, the headlights, and more.

With this one, we need to make sure to remember there is the potential for many layers to show up, but the good news is that the more layers we are able to go through with our images, the more accurate the predictions are going to be overall. If your neural network can make some accurate predictions, then it is going to be able to learn this lesson and will hold onto it along the way and will get faster and more efficient at making the predictions later on.

The neat thing that happens when we are working with these neural networks is that they are able to remember some of the work that they have done in the past. So, if you present the neural network with a picture of a car, and it makes the prediction that the image in that picture is a car, it will remember this information later, similar to what the human mind can do.

Then, if you present it with a picture of a car, especially if this new image is similar to the one that you showed to the algorithm earlier, it is going to remember what it learned before. The algorithm will get through the various layers of the image really quickly and can give a prediction of a car in much less time than before. And this process continues on, with the neural networks getting better at predictions the more times that it is able to go through the information and try out its skills. Just think about all of the ways that we would be able to work with this kind of technology, and this algorithm, to get some of our machine learning algorithms done and taken care of.

Chapter 7: Validation and Optimization Techniques

Now that we have taken a look at a few of the different algorithms that go with machine learning, it is time for us to take a look at some of the ways that we can make these algorithms a little bit better. We would be looking at the validation of the algorithm to make sure that it is working the way that we want, and then, we will focus on how to optimize the techniques that we are working on so that we get the best predictions and insights that we are able to get out of those algorithms. So, let's dive in and see what we are able to do with some of these techniques to make them work for our needs.

Cross-Validation Techniques

The first validation technique that we need to work with is known as the cross-validation technique. We are going to work on our machine learning algorithms here, and at the same time, we are going to take our set of data and divide it into three parts. We are going to have the set for training, the set for validation, and the set for testing.

The training set is the first one that we will look at. This is the one that we are going to use to help train the model. We will want to put about 60 percent of the data that we have available to work on training the model to make sure that it is ready to go.

Then we are going to work with the data set that handles the validation. Once we have been able to select out a model that can perform well with the training set, it is time to run the model with our validation set. This is going to be a small subset of the data, and it is usually going to range from 10 to 20 percent of the data that you have. This set is going to help us with these models because it is going to give us an evaluation, without bias, of the fitness of the model. If the error on the data set for validation increases, then it is possible that we are working with a model that overfits.

And finally, we have the test data set. This is going to be new data that has never been used in training at all. This is going to be a bit smaller, but it is going to contain about 5 to 20 percent of the set of data that we have, and it is meant to help us test out the model evaluation that we are working on to see whether it is accurate or not.

In some cases, there is going to be training and a test set, and the programmer is not going to work with any validation set. There are some issues with this one, though. Due to the sample variability between the test set and the training, the model is going to provide us with a better prediction on the data that we train but will fail to generalize on the test data. This can make us deal with a low error rate during training, but a high rate of an error on the testing phase of this process.

When we go through and split out the set of data that we have into training, test, and validation set, we are going to work with just a subset of data, and then we will know when it is possible to train on fewer observations of the model are not going to perform well, and then we will see that it is going to give us an overestimated test error rate.

To help us solve both of these issues, we are going to work with cross-validation. This is technique involves partitioning the data so that it all goes into subsets. This allows us to train the data on one of the subsets, and then we will use the other one to help us to evaluate the performance of the model that we are working with as well.

To help us out here and to make sure that we reduce how much variability shows up in our data, we may go through and perform many rounds of this cross-validation, but we are going to do this with different subsets of the same data. We can then combine the validation results form these rounds in order to come up with a good estimate of the predictive performance that we are going to be able to get from that model. The cross-validation then is going to provide us with an estimate of the performance of the model that is more accurate than just training once and then assuming it is all going to work.

With this in mind, there are going to be a few different techniques that we are able to see with cross-validation, and these are going to include:

1. Leave one out cross-validation or LOOCV: In this one, we are going to take our set of data and divide it into two pairs to work on. In the first part, we are going to have a single observation, which is going to be the test data. And then, in the second one, we are going to have all of the other observations that come in our set of data, and these will form up our training data.

   a. There are a few advantages to working with this one. First, we are going to find that there is far less bias because we are going to use all of the set of data for training compared to some of the validation set approach where we are only working with part of the data to help with training.

   b. There isn't going to be any randomness in the training or the test data because we will perform this many times, and it will still give us the same results.

c. There are some disadvantages that come with this one as well. For example, MSE is going to vary as the test data is going to work with just one single observation. This sometimes adds some variability to work. If the data point that you work with ends up being an outlier, then you will find that the variability is going to be much higher.

d. The execution of this model is going to be more expensive than some other options because the model has to be fitted n times rather than just once or twice.

2. K Fold cross-validation: This is going to be a technique of cross-validation that is going to take the set of data and randomly divide it into k groups or folds that are similar in size. The first fold that you have is going to be used for testing, and then the model is going to be trained on k-1 folds. The process is going to be repeated K amount of times, and each time that you do, this will have a different group of the data that you will use for validation.

a. There are a few advantages that come with this one. First, the computation time is going to be reduced as we go through the process 10 times, or less, depending on what value you give to k.

b. This one is also going to have a reduced bias, so you can rely on the information that you have more.

c. Every point of data gets to be tested just once and is used in training the k-1 times.

d. The variance of the resulting estimate is going to be reduced the number of times that k increases.

e. There are some disadvantages of k fold or the 10-old cross-validation. The training algorithm, compared to some of the other options, is going to be computationally intensive because the algorithm has to start over again and rerun from scratch k times to be effective.

3. Then we can work with the stratified cross-validation. This is a technique where we rearrange the data in a manner that each fold is going to be a proper representation of the set of data it is going to force the process so that each fold has to have at least m instances of each class. This type of approach is going to ensure that one class of data will not be over-represented, especially when the variable you are using as the target is not balanced well.

    a. For example, we may work on a binary classification problem where we would like to predict if a person on the Titanic was a survivor or not. We are going to have two classes here; the passenger either survives or doesn't survive. We will then ensure that each fold is going to have a percentage of passengers who survived, and another percentage of the passengers who did not make it.

4. The time-series cross-validation: Splitting up the time series that you have in a random manner is not going to help out as much because the time-related data is going to get all messed up. If we are working on predicting the prices of the stocks and then we randomly split up the data, this is just going to make things difficult. This is why we would want to work with a time series cross-validation. In this one, each day is going to be a test data, and then we would consider the data that we had from the day before as part of our training set.

a. We can start by training out the model with a minimum number of observations, and then we will use the data for the next day to help test the data. And we keep moving through this set of data. This will ensure that we are able to consider the time-series aspect that comes with this prediction.

Hyperparameter Optimization

One thing that we need to spend a bit of time looking at is the idea of hyperparameters. These are properties that are specific to the model that we are working with, ones that are going to be fixed even before we have a chance to train or test the data that we have with the model.

We are able to see one of these examples when we are working with a random forest. The hyperparameter is going to include the number of decision trees that we are able to find in our forest to start with. When working with the neural network, there is going to be a learning rate, the number of layers that are hidden, the number of units that we would like to see come with each layer, and a variety of other parameters along the way.

When we bring up the topic of hyperparameter tuning, we are talking about nothing outside of searching for the right set of hyperparameters in order to achieve the high precision and accuracy that we want. When we optimize these hyperparameters, it is going to end up being one of the trickiest and often one of the hardest parts of building a model up with machine learning.

The main aim that a programmer is going to have when it comes to tuning their hyperparameters is to find the sweet spot. This sweet spot in the parameters of the model is important because it ensures that we are able to get the best performance on our project as possible. There are going to be a few techniques that we can use for the parameter tuning, but we are going to focus on the grid search and the random search in the next section because these are the most widely-used options for parameter optimizing.

Grid and Random Search

The final thing that we are going to focus on in this chapter is the idea of the grid search versus the random search. This will help us to figure out which of the two is going to be better for the work that we want to accomplish. Before we look too much into this though, we need to review the hyperparameter optimization that we talked about earlier, because this is going to be important to some of the work that we are trying to do in this section.

First, we are going to take a look at grid searching. This is where we are going to try every combination of a present list of values of the hyperparameters, and then we are going to do an evaluation of the model with each of these combinations. The pattern that we will follow on this one is going to be similar to what we are able to see with a grid because each of the values is going to be placed into the matrix. Each set of parameters can then be taken into consideration, and we will note the accuracy. Once all of the combinations are evaluated, the model that has the set of parameters that provides us with the most accurate overall is considered the best one to work with.

While this is still a pretty straightforward option to work with, one of the biggest issues that we are going to face with it is when it comes to dimensionality; it is going to suffer when the number of these parameters starts to grow. With as few as four parameters in place, the problem can almost be impractical because the number of evaluations that we need to try to work on with this strategy is going to increase. And when we add in more of these parameters, the dimensionality is just going to make the problem worse.

There are times when we are going to use the grid search, but keep in mind that there are times when it is going to take too long and be too complex. This is when we will work with a random search. This is going to be a technique where some of the random combinations of the hyperparameter are going to be used to help us find the best solution for the model that we have built.

In many cases, this search is going to go through the information and will try out some combinations that are random for the range of values. To help optimize this random search, the function is going to be evaluated at some number of random configurations of the parameter space, as well.

The chances of finding an optimal parameter that you can use are going to be quite a bit higher with the random search because the pattern is going to be rained on the optimized parameters without needing to know any aliases. Random search is going to work the best when we have lower-dimensional data since the time that is taken to find the right set for this is going to be less when you have less iteration to work with.

In many cases, the random search is going to be the best technique here, especially when we have fewer dimensions to work with. There are going to be many practical and theoretical concerns when evaluating these strategies. The strategy that is best for your particular problem, though, is going to be one that finds the best value for the fastest and with the fewest function evaluations and it is possible that this is going to vary one problem to the next.

While it is less common in machine learning than the grid search, this random search is going to show us that we are able to get equal, and sometimes better, values compared to the grid search within fewer evaluations of the functions for some of the problems that we try to work with. You have to decide which method you think is the best for the kind of project that you want to work with at the time.

Chapter 8: Unsupervised Machine Learning with Clustering

Unsupervised machine learning is going to be able to help us out with a variety of problems as we handle some of our algorithms. There are times when we need to go through and sort some of the data we have, and we want to be able to make the machine do the work. Being able to handle clustering is a great way to work with unsupervised machine learning because this ensures that we are able to really see where some of our data points lie and can show us some of the hidden insights and predictions and patterns that are there, many of which we did not know about ahead of time. Some of the unsupervised machine learning options that you can do along with clustering will include:

K-Means Clustering

The first type of unsupervised machine learning that works with clustering is going to be the K-means clustering. This clustering is a good way to take care of all the different data points that we have, and see where they are going to be grouped together. You can choose how many groups of clusters you would like. If you are working with separating your customers into genders, then you may only have two clusters. But when you are working with the ages of the customers or even the geographic regions of the customers, then you may end up with five or more clusters.

The idea that comes with this one is that any of the data points that are in the same cluster are going to be closely related to one another. They are not going to have a lot of similarities to the other points that are in the other clusters that you have. This is important because it allows us to see where all of the points of data are going to be placed and will ensure that we are going to see the best results with this in no time at all.

One place where you may see this data clustering happening is when we are working with data mining. This data mining will really work with the clustering if it is more exploratory in nature. You can also work with clustering in other fields based on what we are trying to find out, such as with pattern recognition, lots of machine learning, image analysis, and computer graphics.

The K-Means clustering algorithm is going to form some clusters in your data based on how similar the data values will be. You can then go through and specify what you would like the value of K to be. The value of K is basically going to be the number of clusters that you would like to separate your data out into. The algorithm will be able to help you from here by selecting the center point for your clusters so that the data points fit in.

Then there are going to be three steps that the algorithm will need to go through including:

1. You will want to start with the Euclidian distance between each data instance and the centroids for all of the clusters.

2. Assign the instances of data to the cluster of centroid with the nearest distance possible.

3. Calculate the new centroid values, depending on the mean values of the coordinates of the data instances from the corresponding cluster.

To work with this kind of process, we have to make sure that we can go through and figure out how many clusters we would like to have in the first place. This helps to tell the algorithm where to place all of your data points, and when you print off the visual that goes with this, you will find that it can really help you to see where the data is going to fall, and how all of the different points are meant to go with one another as well. You may even be able to look at this to find a new cluster, and figure out a new market or a new customer base to organize with as well.

There are a lot of different things that we are able to do when it comes to working with the K-means clustering algorithm, but one of the things that we are going to spend some time looking at here is information and the codes that we need to focus on in order to figure out and add in the soft k-means to our code.

Now that we know a bit about the k-means algorithm in general, and we know some of the different ways that we are able to make this work for our needs, it is time to actually take some of these skills and use some Python code in order to make this algorithm work in machine learning. And implementing the soft k-means and the code that we will have below is one of the best ways to make this happen.

To get started with this process, we need to make sure that we start out with some of the standard imports and libraries that are needed, and that we have the utility functions in place as well. This is important because it is going to help us to get something similar to the Euclidean distance, and the cost function going together. The syntax of Python code that we are able to use with this one will include the following:

```
import numpy as np
import matplotlib.pyplot as plt


def d(u, v):
```

```
    diff = u - v
    return diff.dot(diff)


def cost(X, R, M):
    cost = 0
    for k in xrange(len(M)):
        for n in xrange(len(X)):
            cost += R[n,k]*d(M[k], X[n])
    return cost
```

After this part, we are going to take the time to define your function so that it is able to run the k-means algorithm before plotting the result. This is going to end up with a scatter plot where the color will represent how much of the membership is inside of a particular cluster. We would do that with the following code.

```
def plot_k_means(X, K, max_iter=20, beta=1.0):
    N, D = X.shape
    M = np.zeros((K, D))
    R = np.ones((N, K)) / K
```

```python
# initialize M to random
for k in xrange(K):
    M[k] = X[np.random.choice(N)]

grid_width = 5
grid_height = max_iter / grid_width
random_colors = np.random.random((K, 3))
plt.figure()

costs = np.zeros(max_iter)
for i in xrange(max_iter):
    # moved the plot inside the for loop
    colors = R.dot(random_colors)
    plt.subplot(grid_width, grid_height, i+1)
    plt.scatter(X[:,0], X[:,1], c=colors)

    # step 1: determine assignments / resposibilities
    # is this inefficient?
    for k in xrange(K):
        for n in xrange(N):
            R[n,k]  =  np.exp(-beta*d(M[k],  X[n]))  /
np.sum( np.exp(-beta*d(M[j], X[n])) for j in xrange(K)
)

    # step 2: recalculate means
```

```
        for k in xrange(K):
            M[k] = R[:,k].dot(X) / R[:,k].sum()


        costs[i] = cost(X, R, M)
        if i > 0:
            if np.abs(costs[i] - costs[i-1]) < 10e-5:
                break


    plt.show()


def main():
    # assume 3 means
    D = 2 # so we can visualize it more easily
    s = 4 # separation so we can control how far apart
the means are
    mu1 = np.array([0, 0])
    mu2 = np.array([s, s])
    mu3 = np.array([0, s])


    N = 900 # number of samples
    X = np.zeros((N, D))
    X[:300, :] = np.random.randn(300, D) + mu1
    X[300:600, :] = np.random.randn(300, D) + mu2
    X[600:, :] = np.random.randn(300, D) + mu3
```

```python
# what does it look like without clustering?
plt.scatter(X[:,0], X[:,1])
plt.show()


K = 3 # luckily, we already know this
plot_k_means(X, K)


# K = 5 # what happens if we choose a "bad" K?
# plot_k_means(X, K, max_iter=30)


# K = 5 # what happens if we change beta?
# plot_k_means(X, K, max_iter=30, beta=0.3)



if __name__ == '__main__':
    main()
```

Hierarchal Clustering

Along the same idea is the K-Means clustering, we also need to take a look at a method that is known as the hierarchal clustering. In statistics and data mining, this is going to be a method of analyzing clusters, where we are going to work to build up a hierarchy of clusters. There are going to be a few strategies that we are able to use to handle this kind of clustering, but often they are going to fall into one of two types, including:

1. **Divisive**: This is going to be the top-down approach. This will include how all of the observations that you are using will start out in one cluster, and then these will be split up and move down through the hierarchy until you reach the end.

2. **Agglomerative**: This one is going to be the opposite. You will start out with each observation falling in its own cluster, and then you are able to merge together pairs of the clusters as you go up the hierarchy that you are working with.

For the most part, you will be able to determine the splits and the merges in a greedier manner. The results of this are usually going to be presented with a dendrogram.

To help us determine which ones are going to be combined or split up, we need to be able to look for and measure out the dissimilarity between the sets of observations that we are working with. The good news is that with most methods of this kind of clustering, we are going to be able to make this happen with an appropriate metric, which is a measure of distance between observations and pairs, and a linkage criterion that is going to let us know the dissimilarity of sets as a function of the pairwise distances of observations in the sets we are working with.

DBSCAN

DBSCAN is stands for Density-based spatial clustering of applications with noise. This is going to be a pretty well-known data clustering algorithm that is going to be used in things like data mining and machine learning to help us to move our data into clusters so that we are able to read through it and understand better. Based on a set of points, this algorithm is going to be able to group together points that are close to one another based on some kind of distance measurement and a minimum point amount. It is also going to mark out some of the outliers that we have that are found in some of the lower-density regions to help us see where these outliers are.

To keep it simple, we will find that this kind of algorithm is going to come with 2 parameters that we need to know. These are going to include:

1. **Eps**: This is going to tell us how close the points need to be to one another before they can be seen

as part of the cluster. However, if the distance between the two is either low or even equal, these would be considered as neighbors.

2. minPoints: This is going to be the minimum number of points that are needed to form a region that is dense. So if we set this parameter to 5, then we need to have at least five of these points in order to form a dense region.

Then we are able to move on to doing parameter estimation. This is going to be something that we need to focus on for every kind of task in data mining. To choose the right parameters, we have to understand how they are used and then have at least a basic previous knowledge about the set of data that we are going to work with.

For the eps from above, if the value that you choose is too small, then you will end up with a lot of your data not being clustered. It is going to be considered outliers because it won't be able to provide the points. On another point, if the value that was chosen is too high, clusters will merge, and the majority of objects are going to fall into the same cluster. This means that we need to choose the eps based on the distance of the set of data, but in general, going with a smaller value for this is going to be preferable.

We can also work with the minPoints that we talked about before. As a rule, the minimum of this can be derived when we take the data set as minPoints greater than or equal to D + 1. Larger values are often going to be better for the sets of data that have a lot of noise and will form more significant clusters. The minimum value for the minPoints must be three, but larger the set of data, the larger the value that should be chosen.

There are a lot of reasons that we are able to use the DBSCAN algorithm for our needs. This algorithm is going to be a good one to use to find associations and structures in data that might be hard to get manually, but that is still useful and relevant to help you predict trends and find the patterns that you want. Clustering methods are going to be used in a lot of industries, and you will be able to use the DBSCAN to handle a lot of this as well along the way.

Any time that your business needs to work with an algorithm that can cluster together different points, the DBSCAN algorithm is a good one to use, it is a simple idea that you can reverse and do work in more than one method at the same time, and it can really help you to see which points belong to each cluster in no time as well.

The good news with this one is that this is an algorithm that a lot of programmers already use, which means that you will not need to go through and do the implementation on your own. You are able to use one of the various python packages or libraries in order to handle it. It is also able to work with R, Matlab, and Python. This is a also great way to separate out the data points that you have while making sure that you can get it all set up and ready to go in no time at all. When you are ready to put this to work for your needs, take a look at some of the options of clustering algorithms that are above to help you get started.

Chapter 9: Reduction of Dimensionality

Lastly, let us look at reduction and dimensionality. We are going to spend our time working with both the principal component analysis, and the linear discriminant analysis. We will then compare the two in order to figure out which is the best one to work with, and if we would want to work with each one individually or together. Let's dive in and see what the PCA and LDA are all about.

The Principal Component Analysis

The first option that we need to take a look at here is going to be the Principal Component Analysis or PCA. This is going to be one of those techniques that we are able to use with machine learning that will help us to work with the identification of a smaller number of variables that are uncorrelated, but they are known as the principal components that come from a much larger data set that we are working with.

This technique is going to emphasize on the variation of our data, and then it will capture some of the stronger patterns that are found in the set of data. Simply put, we are going to take some random variables out of our set of data, and then we are going to make sure they are not correlated, outside of being in the same data. But we hope to use these to help us figure out some of the strong patterns and predictions that are found in your set of data as well.

This is an analysis tool that was invented in 1901 by Karl Pearson, and it is going to be used in a number of different types of applications, including exploratory data analysis and predictive models. This analysis is going to be one of the statistical methods, and we will be able to use it in many industries, including computer graphics, neuroscience, face recognition, and image compression to name a few options.

The PCA is going to help us take our data and will make it easier to explore and visualize how this will work and what is inside of that data. It is going to be a pretty simple technique to work with, and it is non-parametric.

And when it is used properly, it is going to help us to take out some of the most useful information that we need to form confusing and complex sets of data overall.

This form analysis is also going to focus its attention on the maximum variance amount with the fewest number of principal components as well. This is done to help us learn as much from the data while using as few data points as possible along the way. When we are able only to use a few points of data to get things done, we will find that it is much easier to make some of the predictions that we want, without having to worry about getting confused and lost with a lot of data.

There are a lot of advantages that come with using the PCA, but one of the distinct advantages that come with this is that once the patterns re-found in the data that you are looking for, you will also find support for compressing the data. One will be able to make sure of the PCA to help eliminate the number of variables that you are working with, or when there are going to be too many predictors present in your work compared to how many observations so that you avoid a problem that is known as multicollinearity.

Another thing that you may notice about the PCA is that it is going to be able to relate closely to the canonical correlation analysis, and will even use something known as the orthogonal transformation. The reason that it uses both of these is to help it convert the observations that you are using into a set of values that will then be the principal components.

The number of these principal components that we are going to use in this kind of analysis is going to be either less than or equal to the lesser number of observations that you want to work with as well. The PCA is going to be pretty sensitive when it comes to the relative scaling of the originally used variables.

There are many times when you will want to use this kind of analysis. For example, it is going to be used in any industry that relies on a large set of data, the social sciences, and market research. This technique can also help to provide us with a lower-dimensional picture of some of the data that we originally had. Only a minimal amount of effort is going to be needed when you use this

analysis, even when you are trying to reduce all of that
data that is confusing and

overwhelming into a simplified set of information that you are able to use.

Linear Discriminant Analysis

Now that we know about the PCA, it is time for us to take a look at a Linear Discriminant Analysis or LDA, and how it is going to be used in machine learning in a slightly different manner than the first one that we talked about. In the LDA, we are going to find a well-established technique of machine learning and classification method that is going to be good at predicting the categories that we need the main advantages that we have with this one compared to some of the other classification algorithms is that the model is going to be easy to interpret, and they are good at making predictions as well.

The LDA is going to be used on a regular basis as a dimensionality reduction technique, and this can make it really easy to work with when you want to handle either classification or pattern recognition in some of your programs in machine learning.

The LDA is going to take a set of data cases, which is going to be known as the observations, and will use this as the input. For each of these cases, you will need to make sure that there is a categorical variable because these are responsible for defining the class, and then we need to have at least a few predictor variables, and we are going to see that these are numeric.

Often we are going to be able to take this input data and visualize it as a matrix, with each of the cases being a row, and then each of the variables being in a column. We can think about each of these cases as a point that will show up in the N-dimensional space. N is going to be the number of variables that we are using as predictors. Every point is going to be labeled by its category to make things a little bit easier.

The algorithm that we can use with LDA is going to use this data to help divide up the space of our predictor variables into regions. These regions are a bit more unique, and we are going to label them based on the categories that we can use, and they will have boundaries that are linear, which is where we get the L in our LDA. The model is going to work at predicting the category of a new unseen case, and it can do this according to which region it is going to lie in. The model will be able to predict that all cases that are inside one of these regions that we created are going to belong to the same category. And as long as we trained the algorithm in the proper manner, this is going to hold true.

The linear boundaries are going to happen because we assume that the predictor variables that we are able to get for each category are going to come with the same multivariate Gaussian distribution. This assumption is not always going to be true in practice, it is going to be fairly accurate, and if it is valid like this, then it is possible that the LDA will still be able to perform well and give us the insights and predictions that we need.

In a mathematical manner, this LDA is going to use the input data to help it to derive the necessary coefficients of a scoring function for all of the categories that we need. Each of these functions is able to take as arguments the numeric predictor variables of the case as well. It is then going to scale the variable going to the specific coefficients of that category, as well as the specific output of a score.

The LDA model is going to look at the score that we are going to receive from each function, and then we are able to use the highest score to help us allocate the prediction or the case to a category. We are going to call then the scoring functions, which are important when it comes to helping us make predictions, the discriminant functions.

There are many times when we are able to work with the LDA to help various companies see the results that they would like. To start with, we may find that this can be used with the prediction of bankruptcy. This could happen on accounting ratios and some of the other financial variables. This was actually one of the first methods that were applied to help us explain which firms were able to survive and which ones would enter into bankruptcy.

We can also use the LDA for things like facial recognition. In some of the computerized options for facial recognition, each face is going to be represented with the use of many pixel values. The LDA is able to reduce the number of features that are present in the face to a number that is more manageable before we do the classification. Each of the new dimensions that show up will basically be a combination that is linear to the pixel values, which is then going to form a template. The combinations that are done are going to be known as Fisher's faces, while those that are obtained through the PCA that we talked about before will go by the name of eigenfaces.

Marketing can even work with the LDA on occasion. This can be used to go through a large set of data and distinguish some of the different types of customers and products on the basis of surveys and other forms of data that you were able to collect. These can help us to gather up the data after formulating the problem, estimate the discriminant function, plot the results in the end on a map that we can easily look over and understand in the process as well.

The next place where we are able to work with this is in biomedical studies. This can help us to get an assessment of the severity state of one of your patients and can even give a good prognosis of the outcome of the disease. For example, during the retrospective analysis, patients are going to be divided into groups according to how severe the disease is. Then the results of the analysis, from the clinic and the lab, are going to be studied to help us reveal some of the variables that are different in the studied groups.

When we work with these variables, discriminant functions are going to be built that can help us to classify diseases in the future patient into the severe, moderate, and mild form. This is the same kind of principle that can be used in the biology of different biological groups.

And finally, we will see that the LDA is going to be used to help out with the world of earth sciences in some cases. This method is going to be used to help us to separate out some of the zones of alteration that are there. for example, when we have different data from various zones available to us, this analysis is able to find the pattern within the data and can classify it all in an effective manner.

Comparing PCA and LDA

Now that we have had a chance to talk about the PCA and the LDA options, it is time to take a look at these in comparison to one another. Both of these techniques have a lot to bring to the table and understanding how these are meant to work and how we can combine them to get the best results is going to be imperative to some of the work that we can accomplish with them.

Both the PCA and LDA are going to be techniques of a linear transformation. One option that we are going to see here is that the LDA is going to be a supervised method of machine learning, while the PCA is going to be an example of unsupervised machine learning. This is because the PCA is going to ignore some of the class labels that are there.

A good way to look t the PCA is that it is one of the techniques that you can use that will find the directions of the maximal variance. On the other hand, the LDA is going to work to find a feature subspace in the data that is able to maximize the separability of the class.

Remember, in this that LDA is going to make some assumptions about the classes that are normally distributed and the covariance of the equal classes. This can be important based on some of the algorithms and projects that you are trying to work with along the way.

Many times there is going to be a lot of confusion for programmers when it is time to decide if they should use the LDA or PCA options for their applications. This is often because they are not going to understand some of the fundamental differences that happen between the LDA and PCA. Hopefully, with some of the help of the rest of this section, we are able to get a better idea of how these are similar and how they are separate.

Both the LDA and the PCA are going to be used in the pre-processing step when it comes to problems of pattern recognition and machine learning. The outcome that you are trying to get with both the LDA and PCA is that it will reduce the dimensions that are in our set of data with a minimal amount of information lost in the process. This is going to help reduce the costs of computation along the way, it can speed up how long the computation takes, and can really reduce the issues of overfitting because we are able to project our data over to a lower-dimensional space that will be able to describe the data a bit better.

The main difference that we are going to see between these two is that the PCA is an algorithm that is unsupervised because it is going to ignore the labels of the classes while working to maximize the variance that is able to show up in the set of data. The LDA is going to be slightly different as it is a supervised technique because it is going to compute the directions that are most likely to represent the axes that maximize the separation between the various classes as well.

When we are working with the LDA, rather than just finding the eigenvectors that will maximize the variance of the data, we are also going to have some interest in the axes that are able to maximize how much separation is going to show up between more than one classes. This is important because it is going to help us get this separability to the set of the data, which is something that will be ignored in many cases when it comes to the PCA.

Another difference that we are going to see with this one is that with PCA, we are not going to have the assumptions in place that the points of data are distributed in a normal way. But if the points of data come to us from other distributions, then the PCA is only able to approximate their features through the first few moments. This means that it is not going to be the most optimal options to go with unless the data points are being distributed in a normal manner.

Then we can switch it over to looking at the LDA. IN this situation, you are going to assume that the points of data that we are looking at are going to come to us from two separate multivariate normal distributions that have different means, while still having a covariance matrix that is the same. What this does for us is give us a more generalized method out of the LDA compared to what we are able to see with the PCA.

It is also important to figure out when and how we would visualize the plots that are needed with both LDA and PCA. The plots have been generated for these two algorithms with the help of the Scikit-Learn machine learning library, and with the help of the Iris Dataset. This is a good one to work with because it has 150 images of flowers in three classes, and each flower is going to come with 4 features. You would then be able to work with both of the options above in order to help you to figure out which flower, off of some images that you have, fit into each category.

This is going to bring up the question of when you would want to work with the PCA method and when you would want to work with the LDA method. As we have been going through this part of the guidebook, it may seem like the LDA is going to be the best technique to go with most of the time, but usually, this is not going to be the case. Comparisons will show us over time that the PCA method is often going to be able to outperform the LDA, if the number of samples that are in a class is relatively small, such as what we would be able to find in that Iris data set from above.

However, if you are planning on working with a really big set of data that has a lot of classes, the PCA is not going to work as well with this one, and it is important to work with the LDA method instead. This is due to the fact that class separability is going to be an important factor in helping us make sure that we are also reducing the dimensionality.

One final note before we finish off with this idea is that it is possible to work with the PCA and the LDA together. This will allow you to get some of the benefits of both of these options, without having to worry about some of the negatives with them as much. There are many opportunities when we need to use this kind of option, but it can really add to another level of power when it is time to handle some of the data that we have with machine learning.

Conclusion

Thank you for making it through to the end of *Python Machine Learning*, let's hope it was informative and able to provide you with all of the tools you need to achieve your goals whatever they may be.

The next step is to start working with some of the different algorithms that we have in this guidebook. There are many times when working with machine learning and good data analysis will be able to help your company to see some results. But first, you need to take the time to collect the right data and then run it through a properly trained and tested algorithm to help you get the right insights and predictions that you need.

These are just some of the topics that we are going to explore when it comes to machine learning, and one of those is being able to pick out the right algorithm for machine learning, and figuring out how to put data through each one to make it work is going to be hard.

There are just so many Python machine learning algorithms out there, and many of them sound great that it can be confusing to know how to make them run the way that you want.

This is why this guidebook spent time exploring the different algorithms, and discussed in-depth information about how these work and what you are able to do with each one. The most of common algorithms like neural networks, random forests and decision trees, clustering, KNN, have been discussed as well. When you are done, you will have a good idea of how to work with machine learning and how to make all of this work on your machine learning project.

There are many times when you may decide to work with data analysis or some of the other parts of machine learning, and knowing which algorithms to choose is going to be imperative to this process.

If you found this book useful in any way, a review on Amazon is always appreciated !

Josh Hugh Learning